Early Childhood Governance

CHOICES AND CONSEQUENCES

SHARON LYNN KAGAN
REBECCA E. GOMEZ

EDITORS

TEACHERS COLLEGE PRESS

TEACHERS COLLEGE | COLUMBIA UNIVERSITY

NEW YORK AND LONDON

Published by Teachers College Press, 1234 Amsterdam Avenue, New York, NY 10027

Library of Congress Cataloging-in-Publication Data is available at loc.gov

Early childhood governance : choices and consequences / edited by Sharon Lynn Kagan, Rebecca E. Gomez.
    pages cm
Includes bibliographical references and index.
ISBN 978-0-8077-5630-0 (pbk.) — ISBN 978-0-8077-5631-7 (case) — ISBN 978-0-8077-7365-9 (ebook)
    1. Early childhood education—United States—Administration. 2. Educational leadership—United States. I. Kagan, Sharon Lynn.
LB2822.6.E37 2015
372.21—dc23   2014042495

ISBN 978-0-8077-5630-0 (paper)
ISBN 978-0-8077-5631-7 (hardcover)
ISBN 978-0-8077-7365-9 (ebook)

Printed on acid-free paper
Manufactured in the United States of America

22   21   20   19   18   17   16   15   8   7   6   5   4   3   2   1

Early Childhood Governance

For our adored and treasured nieces and nephews:

Terry Axelrod
Nancy Edelstein
William Goldberg
Noah James Gomez
Troy Andrew Gomez
Sophia Marie Williams
and
Nolan Joseph Williams

Contents

PART IV: THE FUTURE OF EARLY CHILDHOOD GOVERNANCE

Acknowledgments

First and foremost, we want to thank those individuals who contributed chapters to this volume. Their hard work and innovative thinking shaped this volume into what we think is a very valuable contribution to the field.

We would also like to thank Emily Fox for her painstaking work in line editing and formatting the volume. Without her keen attention to detail, we would not have been able to develop such a refined manuscript. We also offer our thanks to Liat "Lily" Segal Graber and Louise Scrivani for keeping us organized during the inception, development, and production of the volume.

Sharon Lynn Kagan, New Haven, Connecticut
Rebecca E. Gomez, Philadelphia, Pennsylvania

Part I

INTRODUCTION AND DEFINING GOVERNANCE

Introduction

Why Governance? Why This Volume?

Sharon Lynn Kagan

Any reader of this volume is likely to ask: Why a book on governance related to the development, education, and learning of young children? And why now? One might further ask: What difference does governance really make and does anybody, anywhere in the world, actually care about it? After all, the topic is dry, somewhat obtuse, and some would contend quite remote from the real work of caring for and educating young children. To all these questions, one might respond "Spot on!" Yet, for decades, researchers, advocates, policymakers, and theorists have studied the phenomenon of governance. With early childhood education (ECE) now garnering social prominence and economic investment, it is time to examine its governance.

Such an examination must begin by defining *governance*, by which we mean the processes and structures that are created to support and organize the work of governments, organizations, and groups. Using this definition, governance can apply to any entity designed to produce outcomes, be it a group of small children playing, a group of tribal elders adjudicating rights, a private equity firm leveraging huge assets, a community organization seeking to provide support services, or a government carrying out its legislative mandates and responsibilities.

More often than not, however, the term *governance* is associated with the way governments organize themselves to function. Governance typically involves laws, policies, and structures, along with the resources and functions accorded to those structures. Consonant with this interpretation, the United Nations, for example, considers governance to include the structures and processes that ensure transparency, accountability, adherence to the rule of law, democratic participation, equity, responsiveness to the public, and consensus-building (UNESCAP, 2009). In accord with this definition, governance generally embraces diverse functions (e.g., planning, coordination, resource allocation, quality enhancement), entities (e.g., ministries, departments, commissions), and documents (e.g., laws, policies, mandates, regulations). Governance is both somewhat fluid in terms of how it carries out its functions, and somewhat static in terms of the durable, though clearly not immutable, nature of the entities and documents that give it credence. Governance also varies by what the documents say and what the entities are established to do, and what they are funded or have the capacity to accomplish in reality. In other words, governance exists as both a vision and as a reality, with the distance between the two often being quite great.

Adding burdensome yet intriguing complexity to the governance landscape is the reality of multiplicity; there is never just one governance structure or process. Governance entities exist horizontally, meaning that, at the federal level, countries typically have multiple ministries, with some related to fiscal efforts (e.g., finance, labor, economic development), some to social efforts (e.g., health, well-being, social protection, welfare, education), others to infrastructural efforts (e.g., transportation, commerce), and still others to international relations (e.g., the state). But governance entities also exist vertically, so that the structures established at the federal level often are mimicked at regional or district levels.

As if this weren't sufficiently complex, there are also many quasi-governmental governance structures and processes. To circumvent the burdensome process of establishing governance entities, many countries and fields create structures (e.g., commissions, councils, collaborations) that may or may not have the authority and accountability typically associated with governance entities, but that are often understood to be part of the governance apparatus of a country or state. Some of these are designed as boundary-spanning entities that bridge the sectors essential to comprehensive ECE, notably health, social protection, welfare, and education. Moreover, in many countries, as the public sector increasingly relies on the private sector to carry out diverse functions, private-sector entities take on responsibilities that are typically associated with public sector governance.

Finally, and somewhat mistakenly, governance is often confused with the diverse documents necessary for its implementation. These would be more aptly termed *policy tools*; such documents include laws, policy frameworks, executive orders, and guidelines, among others. In short, there are multiple processes, structures, mechanisms, and documents that are embraced by the often used word *governance*.

Indeed, then, because of its definitional complexity, its multiplicity of processes and structures, and its implementation challenges, some find governance inherently intellectually interesting. There is no dearth of scholarship on this issue, emanating from diverse academic disciplines, including but not limited to political science, economics, sociology, and psychology, and within applied fields such as business, education, health, and social development. But intellectual curiosity is not the only motivation for examining governance. Governance is practical and has social utility. Governance impacts the way governments and organizations carry out their work; governance greases and increases functionality. Organizations, as Tocqueville noted so long ago, enable work to get done, and, by definition, governance frames the way that organizations operate. Complex as it is, the study of governance—be it of governments, organizations, or groups—presents intellectual intrigue and practical utility.

GOVERNANCE IN EARLY CHILDHOOD EDUCATION

Although the importance of governance in ECE has been chronicled for decades (Kagan & Cohen, 1996; Sugarman, 1981), its centrality to ECE is expanding as public commitments to young children increase. Historically, interest in governance was justified as a means to make ECE more equitable, efficient, and coordinated. Still major drivers of interest in governance, these goals are joined by new movements to ensure ECE as a child right, as an elixir to poverty reduction, and as a means to span disciplines (health, education, and welfare) and their attendant departmental boundaries. With new funds being expended and new ECE programs being mounted, concern about how to best administer them burgeons. Indeed, welcome as these new commitments are, they can trigger greater incoherence, inefficiency, and inequity. Recognizing this dilemma, some who have examined systems and governance from a theoretical perspective have issued calls for more conceptual work and empirical research on governance in ECE (Goffin, Martella, & Coffman, 2011; Kagan & Kauerz, 2012). Others who are charged with implementing new programs and governance schemes are seeking information to guide their practice.

Caught in this swirling vortex of change, practitioners and scholars have limited opportunity to stop and reflect not only on what is happening, but also on the long-term implications of such abundant activity. Reflecting the momentum of the era, ECE practitioners often lament that they are "flying the plane while building it." Catchy and reflective of the urgency of the moment, the phrase captures part of the intention of this volume: to document contemporary actions and activities. This volume, however, has a broader mission. It is about pressing the pause button to take stock first of the new structures that are shaping contemporary ECE—in essence, to examine the shape of the airplane. Second, it is about asking the hard questions regarding where the plane is going, and whether there are multiple paths to get there, and with what differential consequences. In so doing, the volume seeks to raise and address difficult questions about destiny and about the forces that drive this field to claim its centrality to the broader social agenda. En route to destiny, there are cascades of interim destinations and small decisions—some of which are achieved with or without long-term planning, with or without an evidentiary or experiential base, and with or without thoughtful anticipation of either implementation challenges or opportunities. In a zeitgeist of momentum, seemingly small decisions made today contour (and in some cases, bind) tomorrow's actions. This book, then, is about this era, about the seminal decisions that inevitably predict the destiny of the ways in which we hold, serve, and honor young children and their families. It is about the precious, foundational years from prenatal to age 8 for children, and about the equally precious, foundational years when ECE is rapidly growing and maturing.

Indeed, the timing could not be more opportune for a volume on governance that provides in one place the latest thinking, most recent experiences, and an honest review of the governance issues facing ECE today and into the future. It is to this end that this volume is directed.

USING THIS VOLUME

Aimed toward blending theoretical and practical dimensions of governance and intended to be immediately germane to the burgeoning field of ECE, this volume includes essays by noted, thoughtful scholars and progressive practitioners. The volume does not espouse a single collective vision; rather, it is designed to give voice to multiple perspectives on governance. It is designed to provoke discourse and to raise honest commentary about the strengths and limitations of governance. To that end, readers should expect to be left with ambiguity, but also to be armed with information to guide their own unique thoughts about governance.

Part I introduces the idea of governance in ECE, and sets the frame for rethinking governance in its contemporary context. Chapter 1 begins this by examining different definitions of governance (including distinguishing governance from systems) and by offering a theory of change that can be used to guide the implementation and evaluation of governance efforts. Elaborating on definitional and conceptual challenges, it provides an analytic base for the volume. In so doing, it cautions the reader to take stock of the way in which today's governance efforts, perhaps immutably, are setting the stage and predicting the destiny of future ECE efforts.

With this as background information, the volume turns, in Part II, to provide an overview of the current status of early childhood governance in the United States. Chapters in this section examine different approaches to governance, as well as different typologies for classifying governance efforts. In Chapter 2, Regenstein presents a classification scheme as one way of understanding the range of governance efforts taking hold today. Gomez, in Chapter 3, provides a rich theoretical perspective that provides the rationale for and explication of different ways of understanding governance. Based on a study of consolidated approaches to governance in three states, the chapter also examines the strengths and challenges of governance for developing and managing ECE systems in two of those states. Chapter 4 (Dichter) provides a reflective discussion of the realities related to implementing new approaches to governance. In providing an in-depth look at the nature of early childhood governance as it is being conceptualized and constructed today, this section sets the stage for a discussion of the impact of governance on the development of early childhood systems.

Because governance entities are designed to reduce the chaotic nature of conventional early childhood service provision, they might be expected to have considerable impact on the development of early childhood systems in general and on the infrastructural elements that comprise the system. In Part III, the volume renders an examination of seven important elements of the early childhood infrastructure, and examines each with regard to the ways in which consolidated governance has positively and negatively impacted it, and, conversely, the ways in which it has impacted governance. Discussed in turn, the infrastructural elements are: (1) quality rating and improvement systems (Tarrant & Schaack, Chapter 5), (2) standards (Scott-Little, Chapter 6), (3) accountability (Schultz, Chapter 7), (4) data systems (Cochenour & Hebbeler, Chapter 8), (5) financing (Grafwallner, Chapter 9), (6) professional development (PD) systems (LeMoine, Chapter 10), and (7) family and community engagement (Rendon, Chapter 11). Each of these chapters inventively examines the ways in which governance does (and does not) impact the topic.

Given the analyses of contemporary governance rendered in Parts I through III, Part IV offers prognostications for the future. It examines the critical issues and challenges that must be addressed as the early childhood field attempts to refine and tailor its approach to governance. In so doing, this section examines potential influencers of governance and examines new ways to think about governance. In Chapter 12, Hibbard examines the importance of leadership to governance. Building on this theme, Goffin and Rous (Chapter 13) raise critically important and hard questions that beg for attention. They question who should govern and who should be governed by an ECE governance entity. In raising these issues, the authors underscore a central mission of the volume, notably, to inspire critical thinking as a prelude to effective action. The section concludes with an epilogue by the editors that summarizes the key lessons from the volume.

In sum, then, this volume seeks to place contemporary governance in perspective by revealing its rationale and accomplishments, as well as its foibles and possibilities. Our intention in editing this volume was to make a consolidated contribution to the field by taking an honest snapshot of where governance in ECE is, and where it needs to go to maximize the incredible opportunities being afforded young children and their families today. We hope the reader will find the volume both retrospective and prospective in orientation, and seminal and utilitarian in focus.

REFERENCES

Goffin, S. G., Martella, J., & Coffman, J. (2011). *Vision to practice: Setting a new course for early childhood governance*. Washington, DC: Goffin Strategy Group.

Kagan, S. L., & Cohen, N. E. (Eds.). (1996). *Reinventing early care and education: A vision for a quality system*. San Francisco, CA: Jossey-Bass.

Kagan, S. L., & Kauerz, K. (Eds.). (2012). *Early childhood systems: Transforming early learning*. New York, NY: Teachers College Press.

Sugarman, J. (1981). *Building early childhood systems*. Washington, DC: Child Welfare League of America.

UNESCAP. (2009). *What is good governance?* Bangkok, Thailand: UNESCAP. Retrieved from: http://www.unescap.org/sites/default/files/good-governance.pdf

CHAPTER 1

Conceptualizing ECE Governance

Not the Elephant in the Room

Sharon Lynn Kagan

Throughout the world, policymakers are extolling the benefits of early education and are placing abundant effort, enhanced resources, and considerable political capital behind their verbalizations. Whether lauding early
learning as an elixir to bolster developing economics, a resource to support
families' increasing involvement in the paid workforce, a fiscal panacea to
reduce governmental dependencies on welfare or justice systems, a mechanism to foster social equity and to assuage education and economic gaps,
or a means to advance children's readiness for formal learning, there is no
question that early childhood education (ECE) has soared to unexpected
and unprecedented policy heights.

Evinced by this amplified public attention, the increased enrollments
of young children in programs and the increased allocations of the GDP of
many nations to ECE suggest a rosy picture—that is, at first glance. Masked
by the flurry of enthusiasm and effort, this appetite for investing in young
children is accompanied by new challenges and opportunities. Although this
is not surprising, as growth always occasions new challenges and opportunities, the sheer volume of largely unanticipated (though welcome) attention
and resources has fueled rapid change. Neither small nor incremental add-
ons, these changes are diverse in approach and herculean in consequence,
revolutionizing the way ECE services are conceptualized and delivered. For
example, ECE is becoming universalized; it is no longer an elective service
merely for select populations, notably the wealthy, working, or "disadvantaged." It is no longer found primarily in developed nations, but instead,
it has been placed front and center on the agenda of scores of developing
nations. And ECE is spanning conventional boundaries and creating diverse
new institutions and institutional mechanisms, so that it is no longer the
purview of any single discipline or department (e.g., health, education, or

social services). In reality, as it has been known and understood, ECE is being metamorphosed.

Within the contemporary context, a number of issues surge to the agenda and need to be considered seminal in charting the future for the ECE profession. Among these, finance and funding, workforce enhancement, monitoring and accountability, familial and community engagement, and systems-building are critical. They have been discussed, debated, and written about, with some receiving more attention than others. One topic, however, has received comparatively less attention with regard to the existing, emerging, and potential services for young children: governance.

In part, ECE governance has received less attention because it is difficult to grasp and it is encased in very basic questions that affirm its general ambiguity: What is it? Is it definable? What does it include? Is, and how is, it visible or manifest? ECE governance has not been accorded much attention not simply because it is somewhat abstract theoretically, but because it looks different from other perspectives so that where one touches it influences one's thinking about what it is. Like the proverbial "elephant in the room," ECE governance looms larger than life, commands space, and is hard to move. Stated simply, ECE governance is considered complex, boring, un-budging, and remote from everyday reality.

To other individuals (including authors in this volume), precisely the opposite is true. Early childhood governance is vibrant, taking on endless shapes and functions. It is definable, comprehensible, and knowable. It is critically important now because, without a focus on governance, today's plethora of efforts are likely to infuse even more chaos in the field (Goffin, Martella, & Coffman, 2011; Kagan & Kauerz, 2012).

Finally, governance is intellectually and practically exciting because it addresses deep-seated challenges and is solution-oriented. Considered in this manner, early childhood governance is both timely and seminal. It is creating for perpetuity the frame that permits the consolidation and growth of early care, education, and learning. Governance, without being acknowledged, is setting the stage for the future of early childhood education, sculpting the ways in which the equity, quality, and sustainably of this emerging field are being solidified. Put simply, governance is important and its time is now.

DEFINING GOVERNANCE BROADLY

For years, the word *governance* has inspired controversy. Webster's dictionary (2003) defines *governance* as the "act, manner, function, or power of government" (p. 605). This conception goes on to define government as the "exercise of authority over a state, district, organization, institution, etc.: direction; control; rule; management" (p. 605). So, on the one hand, governance pertains to government entities, while, subsequently, it refers to organizations and institutions (and whatever else the reader might consider to be included in the "etc."). More contemporarily, governance refers to "all processes of governing, whether undertaken by a government, market or network, whether over a family, tribe, formal or informal organization or territory and whether through laws, norms, power or language" (Bevir, 2013, p. 1). So, irrespective of differences in the universe that is being governed (upon which there is diverse thinking), governance relates to the way rules and actions are produced, sustained, and regulated. It relates to processes and decisions that seek to define actions, grant power, and verify performance (Governance, n.d.).

For the purposes of this chapter and commensurate with the more contemporary definitions offered above, governance is not restricted to government and instead incorporates efforts in the public and private sectors, including partnerships of both. It relates to ways in which *authority* is created and distributed (e.g., the defining/producing of rules and actions and the granting of power), the ways *accountability* is required (e.g., the verification of performance), and the degree to which the entity that governs has *durability*.

DISCERNING GOVERNANCE IN ECE

In the area of ECE, governance is often confused with allied terms: *systems* and/or *infrastructure*. It is also confused with the elements that compose governance: its functions, structures, and tools. To distinguish among all these terms, this section provides some helpful definitions.

Distinguishing Systems, Infrastructure, and Governance

As presented in Kagan and Cohen (1996), the early childhood system is a complex interplay between the *direct services* that children receive and the *infrastructure* that supports those services. It is represented by the simple formula: *direct services + infrastructure = a system*. Included in direct services are those received by young children and their families, including, but not limited to: pre/perinatal health and education services to parents, home visiting, family child care, center-based services (including prekindergarten, nursery schools, and Head Start), transition services, and pre-K–3rd-grade efforts.

But these services do not exist in isolation; they are accompanied by a host of supports that, when taken together, comprise the infrastructure. This infrastructure is composed of seven "gears," all of which must be in place in order for the infrastructure to function: (1) governance; (2) finance; (3) program quality; (4) professional development for personnel; (5) accountability, including data and functions; (6) family and community engagement; and (7) linkages with other institutions, including schools. If we take away any of the seven infrastructural elements (gears) or the programs, we cannot have a functional system, as represented by the formula $8\text{-}1 = 0$. To reiterate, a system is the umbrella term that embraces the infrastructure, with one (of the seven) infrastructural elements being governance. This suggests that governance, while being an essential element of the system, is not the same as a system. It is a subsystem, replete with its own properties: functions, structures, and tools.

The Functions of Governance

Currently being debated, the functions of governance are its central property. Presently, most scholars and practitioners suggest that governance functions include, at a minimum, planning, coordination, resource allocation/distribution, public outreach, quality enhancements, and some form of accountability. Demonstrating the currency of the topic, at a 2014 meeting sponsored by the National Governors Association, the functions of governance were broadened to include: Within field ECE coordination/alignment, policy coordination/alignment between ECE and other agencies, sustainability, efficient use of resources, accountability, elevating leadership agenda, and the promotion of state-local collaboration (NGA, 2014). Elaborating further, Gomez (2014), in discussing the principal functions of governance, suggests that they include: allocation (of fiscal and human resources), accountability (compliance, consistency, data), collaboration (within the entity, across external entities), and planning (programmatic and fiscal). She also defines functions that pertain to specific elements, including regulating (licensure, certification), outreach and engagement (families, communities, policy), improving quality (program and workforce), and setting standards (program, professional, licensing). Although there is not presently a consensus on the precise governance functions, it is clear that the functions: (1) are operational tasks taken on by a governance entity; (2) need to be specified; and (3) should include, at a minimum, responsibilities related to planning/coordination, quality enhancement, accountability, resource allocation, and public outreach.

Governance Structures

Governance does not simply happen; it needs a structure to encase its functions, and such a structure often manifests as a public agency or entity. Much like the functions themselves, ECE governance structures also vary considerably and are currently being debated and forged. An analysis done by the Early Learning Challenge Technical Assistance (ELCTA) notes that states that received important systems-building funding via the Race to the Top–Early Learning Challenge Fund vary dramatically in their structures, most specifically in the number of major agencies that administer early childhood programs. The report (2014) noted, for example, that in no state was all governance for early childhood consolidated into one agency; of the 14 states analyzed, five states' early childhood efforts were administered by two agencies; in six states, the efforts were administered by three agencies; in two states, four agencies administered the programs and services; and, finally, in one state, early childhood was administered by five state agencies. The report also delineates which early childhood programs and services fall under differing agency auspices. Such distributions of responsibility, even among so few leading states, reveal the diverse ways in which states are structuring their ECE governance and administration.

To complicate matters further, governance structures are not only limited to public-sector entities. Increasingly, governance is being carried out by new players, with different functions being devolved to nongovernmental entities, often third-party players, over which governments have decreasing authority and accountability (Salamon, 2000). Highly diverse in intent, these structures may carry out supportive, similar, or, in some cases, redundant functions with governmental structures. They may or may not be legitimated in law, may have permanent or durable funding, and may be staffed with multiple paid or voluntary personnel. These diverse governance structures play a key role in the design, delivery, popularization, and accountability of ECE services.

Just as governance structures vary, so do the classification schemata being used to describe them. One prominent schema (described in Chapter 2) suggests that there are three primary forms (structures) of governance: coordinated, consolidated, and created. In the first, coordinated governance, state and municipal entities work collaboratively with one another, but do not imbue an entity with statutory authority; rather, the coordinated work is carried out through memorandums of understanding or through interagency agreements. It is not uncommon to see public–private sector partnerships take hold within this structure. In consolidated governance, early childhood authorities are housed in one principal executive branch agency. This may occur by the movement of disparate programs into the single agency or via the joint administration of a new office by two executive agencies. Finally, created governance refers to the establishment of an entirely new agency devoted to ECE.

Another classification schema, presented at the National Governors meeting, suggests four governance forms: (1) a stand-alone agency, (2) consolidation within an existing agency, (3) a bridge governance structure that sits under two or more agencies, and (4) the traditional or coordinating entity (NGA, 2014).

Governance Tools

Just as ECE governance functions and structures have begged for definitional clarity, so do governance tools. Although still somewhat murky, governance tools are well documented in the literature, often with a focus on their different intentionalities (Lowi & Ginsberg, 1994; Salamon, 2002; Tucker, 2013). In general, policy tools are the key instruments that are developed to execute governance. Divided into two main categories, there are legal tools (laws, regulations, contracts, licenses, permits, hortatory policies) and fiscal tools (vouchers, subsidies, cash transfers, social regulations, tax expenditures, loan guarantees). These instruments or devices fill different purposes and are used separately, or in combination, to achieve policy goals. Two things are important to note about ECE policy tools: First, a vast number of these tools are already in use. Not only are they administered through established governance structures, but sometimes separate early childhood agencies are created to execute a single policy tool (e.g., a voucher program). Second, it is critical to understand that at the very time ECE is defining new functions and reorganizing and/or creating governance structures, it is expanding its use of diverse policy tools. This means that three major shifts related to governance are happening concurrently: The *functions* of ECE governance are being defined; the *structures* of early childhood governance are being reshaped, and the *tools* being used to carry out ECE governance are increasing in number and use. Combined, this makes for a complex governance context.

GUIDING EMERGING IDEAS ABOUT ECE GOVERNANCE

Throughout the recent history of early childhood education, there has been a tacit understanding that governance is an important vehicle to stem the fragmentation that characterizes the field. Not only can governance entities mitigate the negative effects of highly discordant programmatic approaches, but they can also foster more systemic thinking that respects the inherent holistic development and programming needs of young children.

However important governance has become, and however well definitions regarding its functions, structures, and tools are now being forged, it remains enigmatic operationally. Guidance is needed to help assuage ambiguities regarding *how* ECE governance can manifest in reality and *what* ECE governance actually looks like presently. To that end, scholars and practitioners have looked to other countries, fields, and to the context for guidance. Each of these is reviewed as a prelude to offering a new conceptualization of governance within a postulated theory of change.

Looking to Other Countries for Guidance

Recognizing that the piecemeal approach to early childhood governance is not unique to the United States, global scholars have turned their attention to examining diverse countries' governance approaches. A series of policy studies underscores the variety of governance approaches that exist, with services typically split between two ministries (UNESCO, 2007). Some suggest that the division of early childhood services into multiple ministries reflects the limited value accorded it (Bennett, 2011); if early childhood were truly valued, it would be consolidated and rendered visible by its endorsement as a distinct ministry. Much of this work, and that supported by other scholars (Kaga, Bennett, & Moss, 2010), notes that the consolidation of early childhood services under ministries of education is an emerging trend in countries such as Brazil, Jamaica, Kenya, New Zealand, Norway, Slovenia, South Africa, Sweden, Spain, and Vietnam. Although ministries and functions are not consolidated under education, per se, the Philippines are another case in point; here, a new agency called the Early Childhood Care and Development Council was established as a consolidated lead agency. Examining this effort, Manuel and Gregorio (2011) note that there is still much work to be done, and, although the sustainability of the Council is now in question, its existence legitimated the importance of early childhood to the country. Despite many implementation challenges, scholars have noted that consolidation can improve recruitment levels, training and employment conditions of staff, and the alignment of curriculum (Kaga, Bennett, & Moss, 2010). Split systems often lead to inequities in services, with one of the participating sectors delivering lower-quality and less equitably distributed services.

Consolidating child care and early education under a single ministry (be it education or others) has been a key strategy, but it is not the only one. In Colombia, for example, a multisector commission (Intersectoral Commission for Early Childhood Development [CIPI]) was established to coordinate services across agencies and has achieved notable successes in launching a major national strategy. Called *De Cero a Siempre*, the strategy was launched in 2010 with pilot efforts in six municipalities; it is presently being expanded, with plans to durably instantiate it in law (Yoshikawa et al., in press). Other analyses indicate that governance efforts are being expanded at the country, regional, and municipal levels, noting the various ways the decentralization of governance is taking hold (Britto et al., 2014). In short, international literature bespeaks the importance of addressing governance, offers trends about the inclusion of governance efforts within ministries of education, and points out that multiple approaches are under way.

Looking to Education for Guidance

In the United States, as in many other countries, early childhood services are primarily (though not fully) associated with education. In part, this may be because the very name "early childhood education" includes the word *education*, reinforcing this conception. Such an affiliation with education may also arise because ECE is most often equated with center-based services that often resemble school and take place in school-like facilities. And, it may be that ECE often serves preschoolers in their year immediately preceding formal education, making the links to schooling imperative. Whatever the rationale, the "education" focus of ECE is prominent, increasing, and influential, with many supporting it. Simultaneously, others express serious concerns, noting that an educational focus can lead to premature demands being placed on cognitive development to the detriment of social, emotional, physical health, and language development. Whatever one's stance on education's influence, the rampant trend toward "schoolification," "educationalization," or the close identification with schools as instruments of formal education has been well noted and documented (Kagan, 2013). Discussing the value of educationalization and the schooling trend is not the subject of this chapter; rather, it must be noted because it heavily influences the governance structures that are being put in place.

Presently, many states and countries are using public education as a model for governance and in some cases for funding. In many ways, this makes eminent sense. First, public education is a public good, making its universality unquestioned, a hope that many advocate for ECE. Second, because of its acknowledged importance to the social good, education has durable and fairly transparent governance apparatuses at the state and local levels, something to which the emerging ECE field also aspires. Third, public education has well-established funding that is sustained over time. Fourth, education has a well-developed infrastructure that embraces professional development pipelines, accountability systems, and quality assurance mechanisms—infrastructure elements that are badly needed by ECE. Finally, given that most young children end up in the public education system, establishing ECE governance as a part of the formal education structure, or solidly linked to it, can foster the kind of developmental continuity for children, teachers, and curriculum that has long been desired in ECE. Combined, these factors have led to a burgeoning interest in education governance as a model for ECE.

Yet, many concerns exist. First, many question the wisdom of modeling ECE governance on education governance when the viability of K–12 governance is being seriously challenged. Tucker (2013), for example, in examining education governance in the United States and in many other highly successful countries, notes that the U.S. governance system is failing American education. He suggests the strengthening of centralized state-level governance and a weakening of lay-citizen engagement in favor of more control by politicians, especially by governors who are elected. Others elect to bypass or reduce the role of public governance structures by operating schools in the private sector or by seeking policy waivers that give them more autonomy. Whatever one's stance is on the weakening of lay control, the strengthening of state governance in general, and of education governance specifically, it is clear that the structure and functions of the U.S. governance systems is under examination and, according to many, in need of reform.

Second, from its foundational literature, ECE has never been conceptualized as solely the purview of education. Rather, education is regarded as necessary but insufficient to meet the comprehensive developmental needs of young children. Health and social protection are essential services, as are commitments to families and communities. As a result, many question a close structural and pedagogical affiliation with education, and seek other governance approaches that resonate more proximally with ECE's comprehensive intentions. Many of these approaches involve the establishment of structures that span or embrace multiple departments. For example, one prominent manifestation of efforts to honor ECE's multidisciplinary heritage, while meeting the needs of its diverse constituents, is to create boundary-spanning entities (BSEs) that pull together multiple disciplines.

Such mechanisms may or may not carry the weight of an operational line agency, but BSEs are emerging with regularity, often to support the work of line agencies.

Looking to the Context for Guidance

As informative as lessons from other countries and fields are, as states and municipalities consider their own governance structures and functions, they will need to look to their own context for guidance. With unique histories, cultures, laws, and customs, countries and states differ markedly in how they conceptualize the role of the state, its obligations to children, and its preferred mechanisms and tools for carrying out its social responsibilities.

In the United States, for example, the constitution cedes primary responsibility for education to the states. Despite increasing and much debated federal involvement in education, education (and with it potentially much of ECE) is under state and local aegis. This policy context differs markedly from countries where centralization reigns. The question, then, is how truly relevant is the guidance rendered by diverse states and countries. In reality, the press for functional and structural isomorphism, although well intentioned, may not be either fully desirable or feasible, given the sociopolitical variation that characterizes the governance context. With regard to desirability, contexts vary over time and within time. That is to say that not only is State A different from State B, but State A may have very different predilections about ECE generally and early childhood governance specifically from one time period or one election cycle to another. With regard to feasibility, states also vary in their capacity and motivation to establish governance structures. In the United States, incentive-driven strategies, such as Race to the Top, motivate governance action with fiscal rewards; such rewards, however, are given to the more advanced states that demonstrate an innovative and committed ECE history and capacity. This incentive-driven strategy can serve to reinforce the governance capacity of already top-performing states, while leaving lower-capacity states to forge forward without the benefit of such resources, potentially further fueling diversity of capacity and governance. Whether advanced by current policy or not, approaches to governance are heavily contoured by history and context, evoking governance entities that vary tremendously. No single governance model has materialized, or is likely to (or necessarily should) materialize, in all states or countries. Rather, states need a coherent analysis of the key ingredients and processes that conspire to build effective early childhood governance mechanisms. These understandings, coupled with a nuanced perspective on the unique context, provide the best guidance for formulating functional and effective ECE governance mechanisms.

KEY INGREDIENTS FOR EFFECTIVE GOVERNANCE

The formulation of an effective ECE governance approach rests on two key complementary ingredients: The first is having clear expectations regarding *what* governance can (and cannot) accomplish. This means having a solid understanding of the true outputs that governance can render. The second key ingredient is having a clear understanding of *how* governance works. This means using a logic model or a theory of change to guide the many actions that will ensue under the mantle of governance. Each is described below.

Discerning *What* Governance Can (and Cannot) Accomplish: Systemic Outputs

With increasing attention being accorded to governance in general and to ECE governance specifically, it is important to ask what can be expected of a well-functioning governance mechanism. What are the outcomes and outputs of effective governance, and how do we distinguish among them?

With regard to governance in general, the distinction between outcomes and outputs is significant. Outcomes refer to long-range eventualities that provide intentionality to the mission of the undertaking. Often, outcomes may not be directly or solely attributable to the intervention because they can take a long time to develop and are affected by multiple factors. Outputs, on the other hand, are shorter-range accomplishments that can be more easily and directly linked to the intervention.

In the case of ECE governance, the presumed outcome is the improved well-being of young children and their families. Such an outcome is laudatory, challenging, and is influenced by many factors, some systemic (i.e., service quality and access) and some familial (i.e., income, intention, engagement). However important and worthy, child and family well-being is a governance *outcome*, not a governance *output*.

Having noted this distinction, we need to address, then, the outputs, or the accomplishments, that we might actually expect from a well-functioning governance effort. Generally speaking, the existence of any governance structure is not the end, the outcome, in itself. Rather, it is a means to an end, a vehicle that leads to the accomplishment of outcomes. It is, therefore, erroneous to expect good ECE governance alone to produce child outcomes. Effective governance is, however, an excellent conduit to outcomes; it can produce important outputs. In ECE, this means that when governance is linked with the six other elements of the ECE infrastructure (finance; quality efforts; assessments, data, and accountability; human capacity; citizen and family engagement; and linkages), it can produce systemic outputs.

Now, the question is: What precisely are the appropriate systemic outputs that can be expected from an ECE system? Interestingly, while clarity has emerged on the elements of an ECE system, there has been far less attention accorded to defining these systemic outputs, measuring them, and discerning how governance contributes to their production. With that in mind, I offer three systemic outputs that are reasonable to expect from a well-functioning governance system, assuming it is working in concert with other elements of the infrastructure.

- *Equity:* All early childhood programs will be equitably financed and distributed. This means that, with good governance mechanisms and a solid implementation of the infrastructure, we should expect that programs and services for young children and their families will be equitably funded and distributed.
- *Quality:* All early childhood programs and services will be of a quality commensurate to produce the desired outcomes for children.
- *Sustainability:* All early childhood programs and services will be sustained over time.

These three systemic outputs—equity, quality, and sustainability—are the products of the system itself. They can be measured once criteria are established, and they contribute to significantly improving outcomes for children and families. It is these three systemic outputs to which policymakers should hold ECE governance accountable.

No matter how important, however, governance alone will not produce child outcomes. It is just one part of the whole picture. To achieve desired outcomes, we need these three systemic outputs *and* fully functioning parents and families. Enunciating this underscores the long-held developmental principle that parents and families are their children's most important teachers. It is the combination of functioning systems and functioning families that evoke effective child outcomes.

Discerning *How* Governance Works: A Theory of Change

Figure 1.1 graphically explains how the systemic outputs can be achieved. Depicted as a theory of change, it is offered as one approach that can guide the way resources (time, money, and human capital) are used as ECE governance functions, structures, and tools are created. The letters indicated below are keyed to cells in the figure. Informed by institutional theory and complex adaptive systems theory (Duit & Galaz, 2008; Gomez, 2014; Meyer & Scott, 1983), the conceptual framework begins with the premise that sociocultural (values, beliefs, heritages, and religions) [H] and temporal (political, economic, and environmental) [G] variables both frame and contour the context in which institutional policies and programs exist. These are represented in the figure by the outer rectangles that encase the theory of change being advanced. Working backwards, the postulated theory of change suggests that improved child and family outcomes [F] will only be achieved when systemic outputs (defined as equitably distributed, high-quality, sustained services [D]) are combined with family outputs (defined as meaningfully involved and organizationally supported [E]). In order for these conditions to exist, a well-conceptualized, well-designed, effective ECD system [C] must be in place. Scattershot and scatter-funded programs and services cannot deliver equitably distributed, quality services at scale; only a system can do that. To render such a system operational, programs and services (including boundary-spanning efforts)[1] [A] must be supported by an articulated infrastructure [B]. The essential elements of the infrastructure (e.g., gears) must be clear and linked. The first and most critical element of the infrastructure is the governance apparatus because it holds the key to realizing other infrastructural elements.

Working forward, the theory of change suggests that *together* programs/services and the infrastructure (with governance highlighted) constitute the system, which, in turn, has the potential to produce positive systemic and familial outputs that provide the best chance to produce outcomes of improved well-being of young children and their families. From a formulaic perspective, it suggests that: A + B are the requisite conditions that lead to C; when in place, C leads to D and E; and D + E are the precursors that enable the production of F.

IMPLEMENTING EARLY CHILDHOOD GOVERNANCE

Once we clarify the definition and concepts of early childhood governance and specify a theory of change with clear outputs, more cohesive and

Figure 1.1. Conceptual Map

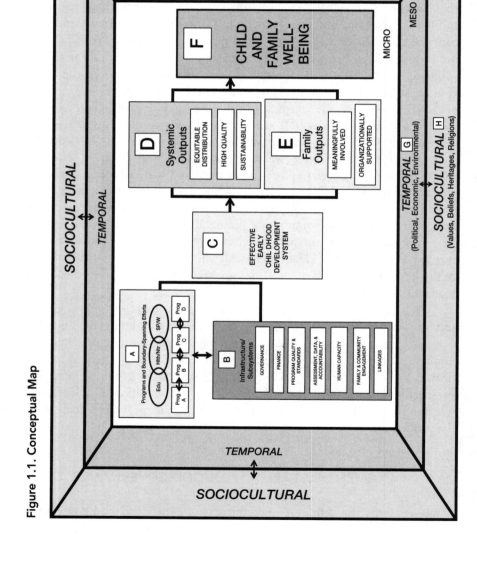

thoughtful implementation can take place. As chapters in this volume indicate, the implementation process does not begin with a huge plunge. The effort required to create new or to modify existing institutions is substantial and one that, by definition, includes dislodging operational programs and people; it must, therefore, be carefully planned and staged.

Planning for Governance

In most states, the planning for a new governance approach begins with a leader, often a political leader, appointing a task force or committee to study the options. This task force is usually made up of representatives of different constituencies who are likely to be impacted by the new governance structure. Individuals who are willing to hear others' views, who are knowledgeable, and who have vision are ideal participants. Typically, successful committees involve members of the business sector, state and local agency leaders, and representatives from the non- and for-profit provider community. Often, the committee or task force planning is led by an external consultant who is perceived to be both knowledgeable and fair.

The planning process usually begins by conducting a thorough review of the services and the agencies currently delivering services. It might also look at budgets and federal regulations, including their constraints and flexibilities. Typically, such a process takes stock of the service delivery spread and who does and does not receive which services. Often, data must be collected from policy offices, extant data bases, and substate units. Analyses of other states' governance practices have been useful in some cases.

Once the lay of the land is determined, the committee or task force, often working in subcommittees, then in plenary, will consider various possible options that comport with the state context. Not uncontroversial, these efforts will demand considerable time and energy to vet, and such a vetting process should be built into the planning timeline and resources.

Leadership is critical in the planning phase, and some states benefit from particularly enthusiastic governors, legislators, and/or business leaders/organizations. Timing the planning process so it does not interfere with political election cycles is desirable, but not always feasible. Communication with the media and with broader constituencies must be considered as well. Finally, and consequentially, a 5- to 10-year budget must be developed, taking into consideration the new expenses that such a governance entity is likely to evoke. As noted elsewhere in this volume, creating a governance structure is not a cost-free effort, much less one that should be sold on cost reductions. Rather, the structure's selling points are the three systemic outputs presented above (equity, quality, and sustainability), coupled with the long-term gains that will accrue once programs and services for young children are equitably funded and distributed, are of high-quality so that positive outcomes will be achieved, and are sustainable over time.

Staging or Transitioning to a New Governance Entity

Once a plan has been developed and a general agreement has been procured, states can launch pilot efforts as a prelude to full-scale implementation. The implementation strategies may vary, but in some cases, the state picks an area or infrastructure element on which to concentrate. Often, this choice is hastened by the prevalence of federal or private incentives. Alternatively, a pilot could be staged so that the full implementation happens in only a part of the state; this alternative may have greater applicability in states where governance is generally devolved to a substate level.

Regardless of whether a pilot is planned, experiences shared by states that have been through this process suggest that a transition plan is helpful in staging which elements should be moved, in which order, and at what times. Typically, states begin by amalgamating a few programs or departments, and then gradually expanding the purview of the governance entity. Fiscal and human resource transition plans are necessary.

As states consider the implementation of their governance system, recruiting and orienting key personnel must be factored in as a significant time and cost variables. Some states have "naturals" who are primed to fill the leadership role occasioned by new governance structures. More often than not, however, because most early childhood training and preparation programs do not focus on preparing leaders to lead systems and to manage governance entities, recruitment can be a challenge. Many systems/governance leaders come from fields other than early childhood, including law, political science, anthropology, and economics.

EVALUATING EARLY CHILDHOOD GOVERNANCE

Once established, early childhood governance must hold itself accountable to its goals. Evaluation data serve both as critical information to enhance the governance structure's performance and also as tools for public accountability. But early childhood governance entities are complex organizations and are notoriously difficult to evaluate. Indeed, very few evaluations have been done, and those that have been conducted tend to focus on the processes associated with implementation (Goffin, Martella, & Coffman, 2011; Gomez, Kagan, & Khanna, 2012). These data are helpful to those who are already committed to the process of developing new governance entities or who are in the midst of such implementation, but they are less helpful to those who need to be convinced of the importance of governance and who want to see verifiable outcomes associated with the existence of a consolidated approach to governance.

There are many reasons that could be proffered for the lack of suitable impact evaluations related to governance. In part, it might be attributable to the comparative novelty and limited number of governance entities. It might be because early childhood research that does not have children or families as the unit of analysis has traditionally been challenging to fund via either public or private resources. Moreover, many potential funders may not fully appreciate the importance of governance, and, hence, have no desire to evaluate it. Further, many funders shy away from anything related to the infrastructure, understandably favoring expending funds on direct services for young children and their families.

Beyond these concerns, there is a host of evaluation considerations that make conducting scientifically solid evaluations difficult. First, the governance entities themselves are highly idiosyncratic, with no two of them looking precisely alike. Some include certain federal programs that others leave out (i.e., Individuals with Disabilities Education Act [IDEA]). Some may function primarily at the state level, while others function primarily at county or substate levels. Some may include a decisionmaking apparatus that is totally private sector–driven, while others combine public- and private-sector actors. Finally, the funding accorded to the governance entities to function directly varies, with some state governance entities benefitting from the Race to the Top–Early Learning Challenge Fund and others not. Indeed, simply determining the unit of analysis is a huge problem, as is finding a group that could fit any single analytic type. Identifying a suitable control group for an experimental study of this kind is next to impossible.

In discerning the input variables, additional complexities arise. In most states where there is a viable governance entity, there is a great deal of change happening in early childhood. Even if some of the changes could be held constant (e.g., Quality Rating and Improvement Systems [QRIS] implementation, or outcome data collection), it would be very difficult to determine precisely which element of the infrastructure is responsible for what change. In other words, attributing the effects to governance alone is highly problematic. Moreover, it is very difficult to envision how one might accord weight to advances in one element of the infrastructure in comparison to advances in other elements: Are common standards more important than a consolidated data system? Is a unique child identifier that is transported with the child across systems more or less significant as an implementation variable than developing a new way to consolidate the regulatory processes across programs? Further, it is difficult to discern which conditions are most accelerative of the desired outcomes, and how such conditions unfold in different contexts. What makes professional development better in one context than in another, or better than data system consolidation? Inherent in these decisions are value metrics that have yet to be conceptually debated, much less empirically determined.

Complicating matters, agreed-upon outcomes that are relevant and attributable to governance have been in short supply. The three key ingredients offered as systemic outputs earlier in this chapter should help advance thinking in this area, but to date, there has been little agreement on whether or not governance entities should be held accountable for precise accomplishments (e.g., budget efficiencies, accrual of personnel savings, streamlined services, and service redundancy elimination), for broader but heretofore ill-defined systemic outputs, or for effects on child and family outcomes. On the one hand, the mega goal has been improved child and family outcomes, but on the other, most scholars have little appetite and less research excitement about using these more distal outcomes as viable indicators of the impact of governance systems. These, however, are the outcomes most requested by policymakers. It is for this reason that the three key ingredients are offered in hopes of rendering measurable outputs of systems work.

Finally, evaluating systems work has been questioned for its social utility. Skeptics suggest that the results from such evaluation might not be used to make changes, given the susceptibility of the findings to political forces. There are those who say that, in the governance game, as in other areas of measurement, it is difficult to measure what matters most, so why, given all the other considerations, expend time and resources on governance evaluation?

Although all these considerations pose considerable challenges, governance efforts are not waiting for the results from empirical studies; they are coming into existence because they seem to make practical sense. Clearly, having solid evaluations would verify (or negate) that premise. Yet, evaluative work is an important area for investment by both public entities and philanthropic organizations because it will shed light on what can be expected from consolidated approaches. Stated simply, despite large challenges, early childhood governance is a worthy endeavor that is ripe for examination not only because it is happening, but because it is shaping the delivery of early childhood services in ways that need to be understood more fully.

CONCLUSIONS

This chapter has tried to do several things. First, analytically, it advanced a thesis that repositions early childhood governance as important, interesting, and infinitely changing, rather than as the boring, immovable elephant whose presence looms large but is ignored. Second and conceptually, it offered a new theory of change, suggesting three concrete systemic outputs (equity, quality, and sustainability). Third and practically, the chapter addressed operational aspects of governance by examining critical implementation and evaluation challenges.

Important for both the present and the future, early childhood governance is generating vibrant new structures and altering the way services for young children are being conceptualized, delivered, and evaluated. In so doing, it is creating a destiny for early childhood education. This chapter does not suggest that early childhood governance is the panacea that will enable the field to live up to the herculean promises expected from it; rather, this chapter asks that governance be ascribed its rightful place as an important contributor to the emerging vision that is being shaped for early learning and development services. Unlike the lugubrious elephant in the room, governance can't and shouldn't be avoided; it is dynamic, vibrant, influential, and it is here to stay.

NOTE

1. See Joachim and May (2010) and Gomez (this volume) for more information on boundary-spanning policy regimes.

REFERENCES

Bennett, J. (2011). Early childhood education and care systems: Issue of tradition and governance. *Encyclopedia on early childhood development*. Montréal, Quebec: Centre of Excellence for Early Childhood Development.

Bevir, M. (2013). *Governance: A very short introduction*. Oxford, UK: Oxford University Press.

Britto, P., Yoshikawa, H., Van Ravens, J., Pongua, L., Reyes, M., Oh, S., Dimaya, R., Nieto, A., & Seder, R. (2014). Strengthening systems for integrated early childhood development services: A cross national analysis of governance. *Annals of the New York Academy of Sciences, 1308*(1), 245–255.

Duit, A., & Galaz, V. (2008). Governance and complexity: Emerging issues for governance theory. *Governance: An International Journal of Policy, Administration, and Institutions, 21*(3), 311–335.

Early Learning Challenge Technical Assistance (ELCTA). (2014). *Early learning governance in Race to the Top Early Learning Challenge States (Rounds 1 and 2)*. Retrieved from https://elc.grads360.org/services/PDCService.svc/GetPDCDocumentFile?fileId=3935

Goffin, S. G., Martella, J., & Coffman, J. (2011). *Vision to practice: Setting a new course for early childhood governance*. Washington, DC: Goffin Strategy Group.

Gomez, R. E. (2014). *Exploring the potential of consolidated approaches to governance for bringing coherence to early childhood education systems* (Doctoral dissertation). New York, NY: Teachers College, Columbia University. UMI: 3621772

Gomez, R. E., Kagan, S. L., & Khanna, S. (2012). *Selecting an approach to governance: Choices related to form, function, and durability*. New York, NY: National Center for Children and Families.

Governance. (n.d.). In *Wikipedia*. Retrieved from http://en.wikipedia.org/wiki/Governance

Governance. (2003). In *Merriam-Webster's collegiate dictionary* (11th ed.). Springfield, MA: Merriam-Webster.

Joachim, A., & May, J. R. (2010). Beyond subsystems: Policy regimes and governance. *Policy Studies Journal, 38*(2), 303–327.

Kaga, Y., Bennett, J., & Moss, P. (2010). *Caring and learning together: A cross-national study on the integration of early childhood care and education within education*. Paris, France: UNESCO.

Kagan, S. L. (2013). David, Goliath, and the ephemeral parachute: The relationship from a United States perspective. In P. Moss (Ed.), *Early childhood and compulsory education: Reconceptualizing the relationship* (pp. 130–148). Oxford, England: Routledge.

Kagan, S. L., & Cohen, N. E. (Eds.). (1996). *Reinventing early care and education: A vision for a quality system*. San Francisco, CA: Jossey-Bass.

Kagan, S. L., & Kauerz, K. (Eds.). (2012). *Early childhood systems: Transforming early learning*. New York, NY: Teachers College Press.

Lowi, T. J., & Ginsberg, B. (1994). *American government: Freedom and power* (3rd ed.) . New York, NY: W.W. Norton & Company, Inc.

Manuel, M., & Gregorio, E. (2011). Legal frameworks for early childhood governance in the Philippines. *International Journal of Child Care and Education Policy, 5*(1), 65–76.

Meyer, J. R., & Scott, W. R. (1983). Centralization and legitimacy problems of local government. In J. W. Meyer & W. R. Scott (Eds.), *Organizational environments: Ritual and rationality* (pp. 199–216). Beverly Hills, CA: Sage Publications.

National Governors' Association. (2014, April). Roundtable on ECE governance.

Salamon, L. (2000). The new governance and the tools of public action: An introduction. *Fordham Urban Law Journal 28*(5), 1611–1674.

Salamon, L. (Ed.). (2002). *The tools of government: A guide to the new governance.* Oxford, UK: Oxford University Press.

Tucker, M. S. (2013). *Governing American education: Why this dry subject may hold the key to advances in American education.* Washington, DC: National Center on Education and the Economy.

United National Educational, Scientific, and Cultural Organization (UNESCO). (2007). *UNESCO policy briefs on early childhood.* Paris, France: UNESCO.

Yoshikawa, H., Ponguta, L. A., Nieto, A. M., Van Ravens, J., Portilla, X. A., Britto, P. R., & Levya, D. (In press). *Evaluating mechanisms for governance, finance and sustainability of Colombia's comprehensive early childhood development policy: De Cero a Siempre.* New York, NY: New York University Press.

Part II

THE CURRENT STATUS OF EARLY CHILDHOOD GOVERNANCE

CHAPTER 2

Glancing at Governance

The Contemporary Landscape

Elliot Regenstein

One challenge for states in developing governance systems is that there is no easy "best-practice" model they can simply adopt. Governance changes take place within a complex infrastructure, and different states have different cultures and values that inform their approach to choosing a governance system model. Because there is no single system that would be right for every state, each state must be thoughtful and choose a model that is likely to be most effective in its context.

To advance an understanding of the different systems of governance, this chapter defines three major system models: coordination, consolidation, and creation. It then identifies the key goals that should underlie any governance system regardless of the model, explains how those goals have led states to contemplate changing their system model, and identifies key considerations in choosing a system model.

GOVERNANCE SYSTEM MODELS

Early childhood governance, in practice and theory, exists across a spectrum of system models—from coordinated governance (potentially including an explicit leadership role in the governor's office), to consolidation of authority and accountability in an executive branch agency, to the creation of an executive branch agency focused solely on early childhood services and programs (Kagan, 2007).

Coordinated Governance

The model of coordinated governance places authority and accountability for early childhood programs and services across multiple public agencies. In approximately 40 states, this is the status quo. States electing to preserve this governance model may seek to improve coordination and collaboration among the agencies with strategies that include formalization through interagency agreements and/or establishing dedicated staff in the governor's office to provide leadership in interagency coordination (National Governors Association Center for Best Practices, 2010). Historically, many states have relied on a children's cabinet or a special task force established by their governors to encourage the coordination of early childhood services (National Governors Association Center for Best Practices, 2010); this type of body provides additional, dedicated leadership for early childhood system work.

Coordination models vary from state to state. For example, in Nebraska, the departments of education and of health and human services co-lead the state's early intervention program and, through a memorandum of understanding, also share planning and administration of quality funds from the Child Care and Development Fund (CCDF) (Nebraska Early Development Network, n.d.). In Illinois, the governor created a Governor's Office of Early Childhood Development to coordinate the work of state's Early Childhood Advisory Council (ECAC) and to support efforts to improve and expand programs and services (National Association for the Education of Young Children, 2011). Ohio's Early Education and Development Office resides within the Governor's Office of 21st Century Education to work with and to coordinate the early childhood work of interagency teams and the state's ECAC (Office of the Governor of Ohio, 2011). In Colorado, a June 2012 Memorandum of Understanding defined a leadership role for the lieutenant governor, working with the state's human services and education agencies (State of Colorado, 2012). And Connecticut's General Assembly authorized an Office of Early Childhood to oversee competitive grants for local preschool programs, in coordination with the State Department of Education (State of Connecticut, 2014).

Consolidated Governance

The model of consolidated governance occurs when the state places authority and accountability for the early childhood system in one preexisting executive branch agency—for example, the state education agency. When moving to this governance structure, a foundational question for the state will be which agency will be designated as the governing entity. This choice can affect the underlying values and principles of future work (Kagan & Kauerz, 2009). States also must be thoughtful about just which services and programs will be consolidated into a single agency.

Three states—California, Maryland, and Michigan (Office of the Governor of Michigan, 2011)—have consolidated child-care funds and state preschool into the state education agency (SEA). Other states have consolidated these services within other agencies: the Arkansas Department of Human Services, the North Carolina Department of Health and Human Services, and the Vermont Department for Children and Families. In Arkansas and Vermont, the preschool program is jointly administered with the state education agency. In five of the six states that have preschool and child care in the same agency, the state's Head Start collaboration office is also housed in that agency; the exception is North Carolina, which houses the collaboration office in its state education agency. Ten states—Alaska, Connecticut, Delaware, Iowa, Minnesota, Nebraska, New Jersey, Ohio, Oregon, and Tennessee—have their Head Start collaboration office in the same agency as state preschool funding, but have a different agency primarily responsible for child-care funding.

Pennsylvania has a unique consolidated model in which it formed a single office—the Office of Child Development and Early Learning—housed jointly within two preexisting agencies, the Department of Education and the Department of Public Welfare. The office is responsible for the financing, planning, implementing, and monitoring of child care, Head Start, pre-K, home visiting, and IDEA Parts B and C (special education), initiatives previously overseen by more than two separate state agencies (Kagan, 2007; Kagan & Kauerz, 2009; National Governors Association Center for Best Practices, 2010; Pennsylvania Office of Child Development and Early Learning, 2012).

Creation of a New Agency

Finally, a state might choose to create a new executive branch agency that has the authority and accountability for the early childhood system. The governing entity thus might be an independent state agency with a single mission focused on early childhood. This type of governance structure requires that the comprehensive set of activities associated with early childhood be situated with the created entity.

Three states have created stand-alone agencies: Massachusetts, Washington, and Georgia. Massachusetts adopted legislation in 2005 that created the Department of Early Education and Care, which has authority over and accountability for early education and care and after-school services for families (Kagan, 2007; Kagan & Kauerz, 2009; Massachusetts Department of Early Education and Care, 2009; Rennie Center for Education Research & Policy; Strategies for Children, 2008). In

Washington, the governor-established State Department of Early Learning serves as a cabinet-level state agency for initiatives that were previously scattered across several departments (National Governors Association Center for Best Practices, 2010; Washington State Department of Early Learning, 2008). And Georgia's Department of Early Care and Learning (Bright from the Start) is responsible for the state's early child care and early education (Kagan, 2007; Kagan & Kauerz, 2009).

CORE GOALS AND KEY PRINCIPLES

There are certain cross-cutting goals that states should address as they consider changing their governance system model. In addition to those goals, there are practical considerations to each of the governance models that affect how successful a model is likely to be in a state. This section identifies some of the critical goals that should undergird the development of any governance system, and articulates the reasons those goals have led states to consider newly created or consolidated governance structures. It then addresses how states may choose to reflect those goals in integrating into the system model existing early childhood advisory councils, regional and local structures, and public-private partnerships.

Goals to Be Addressed in Any Structure

State contexts are different; each state serves different populations, responds to different challenges, and has a unique blend of goals, values, traditions, legal obligations, and political climates. What works in one state and for one governance purpose may not work in another state. Thus, a state that desires to reexamine its early childhood governance system model should not necessarily begin with a particular model in mind but rather with a focus on its early childhood goals and desired outcomes—and then choose a system model based on those goals and desired outcomes (Goffin, Martella, & Coffman, 2011). There are five key goals that states have focused on in their governance design work (Goffin, Martella, & Coffman, 2011; Kagan & Kauerz, 2009):

- *Coordination:* The governance model should connect the different parts and programs of the early childhood system, reflecting its comprehensive nature.
- *Alignment:* The model should provide coherence across system-wide tasks such as data collection, quality standards, and outcome

measurement, and should break down silos associated with the
administration of funding and the oversight of programs.

- *Sustainability:* The governance model should be able to sustain
  political and administrative changes and be designed to best account
  for the full range of programs and services that are part of the state's
  early childhood system.
- *Efficiency:* The model should allocate resources wisely, reduce
  duplication of effort, and provide a significant return on investment.
- *Accountability:* The governance model should be accountable to
  the early childhood system and its stakeholders in terms of quality,
  equality, and outcomes and also should be able to hold services and
  programs accountable for their performance.

Considerations in the Trend Toward Consolidation and Creation

In approximately 40 states, the existing system is coordination, so states considering a governance change are generally states with coordination models that believe a consolidated or created model might better help them achieve their goals. States considering these two models need to decide which model they prefer—and if they choose consolidation, states must decide which existing agency is the appropriate lead for early childhood issues. States considering a change must also confront some practical challenges that must be addressed in any governance transition. Several of the goals identified in this section have been drivers of state shifts toward consolidation and creation.

First, alignment and coordination may be substantially improved by having multiple programs and services under one roof. For example, communication between different programs and services in the field is made easier—so long as the governance entity actually does the communications and consensus-building work to achieve cohesion and alignment.

Second, consolidation and creation models also may be better for aligning accountability with governance authority, rather than maintaining separately accountable entities for separate programs and services (Kagan & Kauerz, 2009).

Third, both consolidation and creation models create higher-level leadership positions within early childhood (e.g., commissioner, deputy commissioner), which may assist the state in attracting better talent to its agency and making early learning a more visible public policy priority—a key factor in the sustainability of public funding.

It is worth noting that states that have adopted consolidated or created governance models experienced disproportionate success in the federal Early Learning Challenge. All three states with stand-alone early childhood agencies

(Georgia, Massachusetts, and Washington) and five of the six states with early childhood in the same agency (California, Maryland, Michigan, North Carolina, and Vermont) are among the 19 Early Learning Challenge grantees.

Choosing Which Programs to Combine. States considering consolidation or creation must decide which programs and services they intend to include in the consolidation or creation:

- Child-care and preschool programs—typically thought of as the primary state-funded early care and education programs—have been a focus of both consolidation and creation efforts.
- Although Head Start is federally funded, Head Start collaboration offices may find it easier to be effective if they are housed in the same agency as child-care and preschool programs.
- Including special education programs with child care and preschool can help further key values of diversity and inclusivity.

Additionally, if professional development supports are housed outside of core program funding, they may need to be transferred into the new structure as well.

Historically, programs that serve 3- and 4-year-olds—such as state preschool and Head Start—have received more public attention than those serving infants and toddlers, but consolidations and creations are an excellent opportunity for states to better connect their work into a birth-to-5 system. Consolidating or creating early childhood programs focused on 3- and 4-year-olds without including infants and toddlers may serve to further isolate supports focused on the youngest children. The programs that reach infants and toddlers may be considered "family support" initiatives and have a more explicit two-generation focus than programs for older children—which has implications for where they are housed currently in state government and how they might be included in a new early childhood division or agency. Moreover, in approximately 20 states, Part C special education services for children birth through age 3 are administered by an agency that does not have responsibility for either preschool or child care. In deciding on a governance system model, states should pay careful attention to the needs of infants and toddlers and ensure that any changes will leave infants and toddlers at least as well off as they were before—and preferably better.

Choosing Between Consolidation and Creation. States choosing between consolidation and creation are generally making a calculation about which model will be more politically effective. Some of the key issues states put into their political calculus are:

- whether an existing agency (like the SEA) or a separate stand-alone agency with its own leadership would have more clout over time;
- whether a small stand-alone agency would be able to advance policy and program goals, and garner resources to support those goals;
- whether consolidation into an agency would lead to the early learning leader being appointed at too low a level within that agency to be a politically effective champion for early learning; and
- whether it is politically easier to create a new agency or to move programs into an existing agency.

The political calculus will differ from state to state, depending in part on the state's constitutional structure as well as its political climate.

Because many of the advantages of consolidation and creation are similar, if it is politically easier to consolidate rather than to create, states can consider a consolidated agency in the short term that could potentially serve as the basis for a spun-off independent agency at some point in the future.

Choosing Where to Consolidate. A central decision for consolidation will be determining into which existing agency the responsibility for early childhood governance should be placed. A state considering consolidation should examine the missions and goals of its existing agencies to seek coherence and alignment of objectives with its early childhood system. States should also assess the dynamics of existing agencies to determine the best fit. Moreover, the state should consider the willingness of the commissioner or chief to take on early childhood governance, as well as the competencies of diverse agencies' staff. Such buy-in is essential throughout the process.

One option is consolidation within the SEA. The SEA is already committed to educational outcomes, and consolidation of early childhood governance into the SEA can ensure a continued focus on early learning—including improving the educational content of child-care programs. For states using a "birth-to-8" frame, consolidation within the SEA may also aid in greater coherence of the continuum of early childhood and K–12 education, particularly in developing learning standards and teacher professional development. The other primary candidate for consolidation will typically be a human services agency. Human services agencies frequently are well equipped to work with the diverse set of community providers that form the core of many state early learning communities.

One complexity is that, in some states, the chief of the SEA has constitutional independence and is separately elected. In these states, consolidating authority in an independent SEA can have both advantages and disadvantages; it can help insulate early learning programs from governors who do not support them, but it can also reduce the level of gubernatorial interest in the programs, which can be a disadvantage in the state budget process.

BUILDING ON EXISTING INFRASTRUCTURE

State early childhood systems have numerous structures that live outside of state agencies: collaborative interagency structures such as regional and local governance structures, Early Childhood Advisory Councils, and public-private partnerships. Although these structures can exist under any governance model, their relative strengths and weaknesses may affect decisions about which governance model makes the most sense for a particular state.

Regional and Local Structures

The three system models are focused on organization within state government, but some states have strong regional and local structures that work with state government. The design of a state system model should take into account these regional and local structures, which sometimes have historically exercised programmatic authority but in other cases are more focused on coordination.

If a state is already heavily focused on leveraging strong regional and local structures, it should consider which state-level governance structure would be most effective at working with those structures. A consolidated or created agency might provide an effective single point of contact for regional and local structures. On the flip side, having strong regional and local structures may minimize some of the challenges that come from having state-level programs spread across multiple agencies.

If a state does not have strong regional and local structures but is looking to build them, it can factor into its state-level governance system the need to develop and support regional and local capacity. Empowering local decisionmakers within their communities may help elevate awareness and support of early childhood issues among policymakers and provide greater visibility among relevant groups statewide. Use of regional entities also acknowledges different contexts and needs within the states' regions. At the same time, states must ensure access to and equity of early childhood services and consider the potential for unclear accountability in regional or decentralized models, particularly where consistency in practice is key to service provision.

Early Childhood Advisory Councils

Regardless of where program authority lies, states coordinate early childhood efforts through a formally designated Early Childhood Advisory Council (ECAC). ECACs are required by the Head Start Act and received startup funding from the American Recovery and Reinvestment Act of 2009 (ARRA). Several state education and human services agencies are required by federal law to be a part of the ECAC. Under federal law, the ECACs were created to play a purely advisory role, although states can vest them with additional responsibilities (BUILD Initiative, 2010). Although the ECACs were created to be advisory, the ARRA funds required them to administer grant funds for projects selected in 2010 and approved by the U.S. Department of Health and Human Services; these grant funds in some instances blurred the ECAC's role.

In the coordination model that most states have used, effective ECACs can provide valuable support to agency administrators (Regenstein, 2008). Changing to a consolidated or created system model will likely change the role of the ECAC; ECACs may evolve into an advisory group primarily focused on meeting the needs of a consolidated or created agency, but may also add value by helping to coordinate the work of a newly strengthened or created agency with other state agencies. Because under federal law ECACs are ultimately accountable to governors' offices, the governor's office should take the lead in defining the ECAC's role in a newly changed governance landscape, applying general principles of successful ECAC operation to the state's new structure.

Public-Private Partnerships

Public-private relationships can play a role in coordinated, consolidated, or created governance structures. Indeed, due to increasing complexities and costs associated with public programming and shrinking state government budgets, many fields (including early childhood) have experienced greater hybridization of the public and private sectors (Kagan & Kauerz, 2009). Public-private partnerships can enhance the sustainability of a governance structure by supporting certain components of the system (e.g., policy analysis, advocacy, communications, public investment and coordination, and so on) and at times can undertake certain roles that are inappropriate for purely public entities (BUILD Initiative, 2010; Ounce of Prevention Fund, 2012). At the same time, states must guard against any conflicts of interest that could emerge.

A state should consider the interplay between its governance system model (whether coordinated, consolidated, or created) and any privatization efforts or public-private partnerships. For example, having a consolidated or created entity to oversee the early childhood system may make engagement with private and philanthropic partners easier because having a clear lead agency for an early learning agenda can help philanthropies understand where their giving is most likely to be effective. It can also provide the opportunity to bring together multiple sectors of the philanthropic community to act in a more coordinated manner; for example, a consolidated or created administrative structure may be able to bring together funders from the education, social services, and health fields, depending on the agency's overall ambit.

Some states have also entered into public-private partnerships—or have supported the creation of a public-private entity—to advance their goals for their early childhood systems. States should consider these public-private partnerships in making decisions about a governance system model, and play different roles within the early learning landscape. For example, Oregon has used ARRA child-care quality funds to support the first phase of an Education and Quality Investment Partnership, a public-private partnership focused on improving child-care quality throughout the state (National Governors Association Center for Best Practices, 2010). In Washington, state law requires the Departments of Early Learning and Social and Health Services to develop a nongovernmental, public-private initiative to coordinate investments in child development, and Thrive by Five Washington is the state's nonprofit public-private partnership for early learning, assembling business, philanthropic, and government leaders to work on initiatives that include family education and home visiting (Kagan, 2007; Kagan & Kauerz, 2009; National Association for the Education of Young Children, 2012; Ounce of Prevention Fund, 2012; Thrive by Five Washington, 2012). And Alaska's Best Beginnings supports local partnerships, an imagination library, and public education and awareness (National Association for the Education of Young Children, 2012).

CONCLUSIONS

Early learning systems serve a diverse population, and any governance structure must provide the infrastructure to serve that population well. In some states, the importance of serving diverse populations has been clearly articulated as a priority of the early learning system (California Department of Education, 2013). Although it should be possible to serve diverse populations in any governance model, states should ensure that whatever model they choose is capable of serving diverse populations effectively.

Finally, it is important for states to recognize that structural changes are only one part of the equation. Changing the structure without changing related practices—rules, procedures, monitoring, and reporting, to name just a few—will mean that existing silos have been moved closer together but not broken down. If the agency staff responsible for the day-to-day management of programs do not end up changing their job practices, then the high-level changes that come with reorganization will likely have little impact on the field. Though this chapter does not explore these practical challenges in depth, it must acknowledge their importance. There is no question that successful governance initiatives require changes not just in where power lies but also in how it is used.

REFERENCES

BUILD Initiative. (2010). *Early childhood system governance: Lessons from state experiences.* Denver, CO: Author.

California Department of Education. (2013). *California comprehensive early learning plan.* Sacramento, CA: State Advisory Council on Early Learning and Care.

Goffin, S., Martella, J., & Coffman, J. (2011). *Vision to practice: Setting a new course for early childhood governance.* Washington, DC: Goffin Strategy Group.

Kagan, S. L. (2007). *Early childhood governance in Florida: Evolving ideas and practice (Final presentation of the Policy Matters Project)* [PowerPoint slides].

Kagan, S. L., & Kauerz, K. (2009). Governing American early care and education. In S. Feeney, A. Galper, & C. Seefeldt (Eds.), *Continuing issues in early childhood education* (3rd ed.) (pp. 12–32). Upper Saddle River, NJ: Pearson Education.

Massachusetts Department of Early Education and Care. (2009). *Massachusetts Department of Early Education and Care strategic plan: Putting children and families first.* Boston, MA: Author.

National Association for the Education of Young Children (NAEYC). (2011). *State early care and education public policy developments (FY11).* Washington, DC: Author.

National Association for the Education of Young Children (NAEYC). (2012). *State early care and education policy developments (FY12).* Washington, DC: Author.

National Governors Association Center for Best Practices. (2010). *Building ready states: A governor's guide to supporting a comprehensive, high-quality early childhood state system.* Washington, DC: Author.

Nebraska Early Development Network. (n.d.). Retrieved from http://edn.ne.gov

Office of the Governor of Michigan. (2011). Michigan Executive Order 2011-8 (June 29, 2011). Retrieved from www.michigan.gov/documents/snyder/EO-2011-8_357030_7.pdf

Office of the Governor of Ohio. (2011). Executive Order 2011-21K. Retrieved from www.governor.ohio.gov/Portals/0/pdf/executiveOrders/2011-21K.pdf

Ounce of Prevention Fund. (2012). *Backgrounder: Public-private partnerships.* Chicago, IL: Author.

Pennsylvania Office of Child Development and Early Learning. (2012). *Annual report 2010–11.* Harrisburg, PA: Author.

Regenstein, E. (2008). *State early childhood advisory councils.* Denver, CO: BUILD Initiative.

Rennie Center for Education Research & Policy; Strategies for Children. (2008). *A case study of the Massachusetts Department of Early Education and Care.* Cambridge, MA: Rennie Center for Education Research & Policy; Strategies for Children.

State of Colorado. (2012). *State partners join forces for children and families.* Retrieved from Colorado, the Office State Web Portal: www.colorado.gov/cs/Satellite?c=Page&childpagename=LtGovGarcia%2FCBONLayout&cid=1251630622101&pagename=CBONWrapper

State of Connecticut. (2014). Connecticut Public Act 14-41. Retrieved from Connecticut General Assembly website: www.cga.ct.gov/2014/act/pa/pdf/2014PA-00041-R00SB-00025-PA.pdf

Thrive by Five Washington. (2012). About Thrive by Five Washington. Retrieved from http://thrivebyfivewa.org/about/

Washington State Department of Early Learning. (2008). *DEL biennial report to the legislature and longitudinal study plan.* Olympia, WA: Author.

CHAPTER 3

Governance as a Lever for Bringing Coherence to ECE Systems

The Adaptive Capacities of Consolidated Approaches

Rebecca E. Gomez

The press for system development in early childhood has been steadily increasing over the past 2 decades. The trend of investing in individual programs for young children and their families persists, but these programs are being created within the context of a burgeoning infrastructure—defined here as an early childhood system. Early childhood education (ECE) systems consist of eight key elements: professional development, accountability, outreach and engagement, quality, financing, regulations, standards, and governance (Kagan & Cohen, 1997). Each of these eight elements is necessary to build a fully functioning early childhood system; however, many scholars and policymakers dispute the relative importance of each element to overall system functioning. Some would argue that standards are the most important system element. Others argue that governance is the most important element of an early childhood system (Gomez, Kagan, & Khanna, 2012; Goffin, Martella, & Coffman, 2011; Kagan & Kauerz, 2008; Kauerz & Kagan, 2012). There are still other conceptualizations of ECE systems that do not privilege one system element over another. In this chapter, I make a case for governance as the most important element of an ECE system by examining the strengths of governance, focusing on consolidated governance in particular. This argument is predicated on the results of a qualitative study that examined the approaches to governance adopted by Pennsylvania and Massachusetts (Gomez, 2014).[1] The results from this study suggest that consolidated governance can yield enhanced capacity to develop the other seven system elements, ultimately leading to a more coherent and functional ECE system. I highlight the unique strengths of consolidated approaches to governance for bringing coherence to ECE systems by analyzing these approaches to governance through the lens of a theoretical framework—complex adaptive systems theory— which illustrates how and why consolidated approaches are uniquely suited to managing ECE systems.

DIMENSIONS OF GOVERNANCE

Governance consists of three dimensions: form, function, and durability (Gomez, Kagan, & Khanna, 2012; Kauerz & Kagan, 2012). An explication of the dimensions does, however, merit repeating for the purposes of contextualizing the material presented here and explaining differences in how these definitions are mobilized in this chapter versus other chapters in the volume. The dimension of form represents the administrative structures in which governance exists—in the preceding chapter, for example, Regenstein presented his conceptualization of the "forms" of governance adopted by U.S. states. The function dimension includes the processes through which the "act" of governing is carried out. These have been articulated in Chapter 1, and include, for example, ensuring accountability, collecting data, and managing finances. Durability, the third dimension of governance, is the degree to which the form and function dimensions can be sustained over time, weathering changes in the state's economic, political, and social context.

Differing from other conceptualizations of governance in this volume, I examine how form and function "interact" to render a state's approach to governance. Several types of governance approaches have evolved in recent years, each with a uniqueness undergirded by state culture and shaped by the interaction of form and function. Some states have chosen to adopt a *consolidated* approach to governance, developing forms that are highly centralized, with the majority of programs, services, and funding streams consolidated into one administrative entity and all functions carried out under the auspices of that entity. Other states have taken a more *decentralized* approach, devolving the authority for some programs and services to the regional or local level. Most states in the United States, at the time of this writing, have a *compartmentalized* approach to governance, with programs, services, and funding streams being housed across multiple entities, responsible only for carrying out functions germane to program oversight.

FORMS AND FUNCTIONS OF CONSOLIDATED APPROACHES

Before discussing the major assets of consolidated approaches to governance in the two focal states of the study, it is important to fully articulate the forms and functions of each. The forms adopted by Pennsylvania and Massachusetts differ greatly, but data from these two states revealed that, despite these differences in structure, they engaged in eight governance functions. These functions could be deemed characteristic of consolidated approaches.

Forms

Pennsylvania created a hybrid structure, the Office of Child Development and Early Learning (OCDEL), into which the majority of ECE programs and services were consolidated. This office has dual reporting obligations to the Department of Public Welfare and the Department of Education. Massachusetts, on the other hand, created a new entity, the Department of Early Education and Care (EEC), into which most of the programs for children birth to age 5 were consolidated. The department resides at an equal level in the commonwealth's structure with the Department of Elementary and Secondary Education and the Department of Higher Education. (An articulation of the precise programs and services that were consolidated into each of these two entities is provided later in this chapter.)

Functions

An examination of how the OCDEL and the EEC engage in governance of the ECE system in their respective commonwealths revealed that their functionality is comprehensive in nature. Both carry out eight major functions of governance; taken together, these functions are arguably unique to consolidated approaches to governance. These eight functions are: (1) *allocation*, both human resource and fiscal; (2) *planning*, both programmatic and fiscal; (3) *accountability*—collecting data, ensuring compliance with rules and regulations, and ensuring that programs are implemented with consistency and (when applicable) fidelity; (4) *collaboration* with other entities within government and outside of government; (5) *outreach and engagement* to/with stakeholders from all sectors of the ECE field; (6) *regulating* ECE programs; (7) *standard-setting* for young children, ECE programs, and for the ECE workforce; and, (8) *improving quality* of both ECE programs and the ECE workforce (Gomez, 2014).

These eight functions are carried out across all programs and services over which a consolidated governance entity has authority. Although they are analytically distinct, these functions often overlap in practice. Allocation of human or financial resources, for example, often requires that a state first engage in planning functions. Another example of this overlap is that a governance entity might engage in collaborative activities with external partners (e.g., contractors) to ensure that they can implement programs with consistency, a subfunction of accountability. A third instance of this overlap is visible in the Pennsylvania and Massachusetts QRIS standards, which supersede the regulatory floor and contain quality indicators that programs meet voluntarily; thus, empirically, the implementation of the QRIS is an enactment of several overlapping governance functions (regulation, standard-setting, quality). These examples illuminate how governance functions are carried out within the consolidated entities: either with the goal of promoting the development of a particular system element (e.g., regulations) or subsystem (e.g., QRIS, which necessitates the interaction of several system elements that include quality, outreach and engagement, planning, and financing) of the state's ECE system.

THEORETICAL UNDERPINNINGS

The presentation of form and functions provided here affords insight into what consolidated governance looks like and can accomplish. Locating ECE systems and the dimensions of governance (i.e., form and function) within a theoretical framework helps further elucidate why consolidation may provide a uniquely robust approach to governing ECE systems.

In this section, using complex adaptive systems theory, I explain why the ECE system is a complex adaptive system. I then turn to an explication of boundary-spanning policy regimes (BSPRs), discussing how and why consolidated approaches to governance rise to the level of a BSPR, and what this means for ECE system management. By examining ECE governance within the context of these theoretical and conceptual frameworks, we can see how consolidated approaches are perhaps a uniquely apt approach to managing ECE systems.

Complex Adaptive Systems

One purpose of theory is to serve as an explanatory tool—constructs from a particular theoretical framework can help contextualize and clarify the data being analyzed. Analyzing consolidated governance in Massachusetts and Pennsylvania through the lens of complex adaptive systems theory helps define and describe the ECE system as a system that is uniquely complex. Complex adaptive systems (CAS) theory is predicated on the notion that certain systems are inherently—as the name would suggest—complex and complicated and, thus, difficult to manage (Snyder, 2013). CAS are characterized by four traits (Duit & Galaz, 2008), each of which is present in ECE systems: (1) agents of change, represented by individuals and organizations who act within the system to change it; (2) self-organizing processes, through which individuals (e.g., policymakers, ECE teachers, families) respond to available information about the system; (3) co-evolutionary processes, by which many agents of change attempt to bring coherence to the system simultaneously; and (4) unstable equilibriums within the system, such as political, cultural, and economic shifts that occur within the broader institutional environment(s).

It is these four characteristics that make CAS notoriously difficult to govern (Duit & Galaz, 2008; Gomez, 2014; Snyder, 2013). Indeed, anyone who has worked within the ECE field could attest to these characteristics, particularly the unstable equilibriums that stem from financing challenges, low program quality, lack of access, and lack of equity. Given these realities, conceptualizing ECE systems as complex adaptive systems has considerable implications for governance. In particular, it is important to identify which types of approaches to governance might yield effective management of a complex system that is, by definition, difficult to govern.

To understand the ways in which consolidated governance is uniquely positioned to manage the complexities of the ECE system, it is important to understand the nature of consolidated governance—that is to say, it is important to understand the ways in which form and function interact to yield a high capacity for system management.

Boundary-Spanning Policy Regimes

Consolidated approaches to governance provide the necessary tools for managing and bringing coherence to CAS, because they possess two characteristics that foster policy integration: a high degree of authority and a broad scope. These two characteristics render consolidated approaches a type of boundary-spanning policy regime (BSPR). BSPRs are a type of "governing arrangement that spans multiple subsystems and fosters integrative policies" (Joachim & May, 2010, p. 307), and transcend a set of loosely collated subsystems. In their discussion of BSPRs in practice, Joachim and May (2010) cite the Drug Enforcement Agency (DEA), created in response to President Reagan's "war on drugs," as an example of a BSPR created to foster an integrated national drug policy. The DEA was imbued with the authority to act and with a broad scope of jurisdiction. The findings related to form and function in Pennsylvania and Massachusetts reveal that both entities have a high degree of authority over the ECE system and a broad scope—both vertically (ages served) and horizontally (types of programs under the auspices of the EEC and OCDEL). These findings are in contrast to the conditions present prior to consolidation in these two commonwealths, in which the ECE system existed as a set of loosely collated subsystems under the authority of several different government departments or offices.

Defining consolidated approaches to governance as BSPRs is useful in that it expands the field's conceptual "map" of what governance is and what it can do. It also provides insight into the relative capacity of consolidated approaches to manage complex adaptive systems, such as ECE systems. The EEC and OCDEL have a high degree of authority and a broad scope of jurisdiction in which they carry out governance functions. This renders these entities both powerful and flexible, enabling them to effectively manage the ECE system even in the face of exogenous political and economic forces.

Notably, both the EEC and OCDEL have survived political and economic shifts (often resulting in unstable equilibriums in the ECE system) since their inception. Study participants felt that the functionality of these entities was largely responsible for their durability—the third dimension of governance in the face of these changes (Gomez, 2014).

Authority as a Regime Characteristic. Authority is the first characteristic of a BSPR, and the first example of how form and function interact: The consolidated entity in the focal states is imbued with the authority to carry out the functions of governance across the majority of the ECE system. Prior to consolidation in Massachusetts and Pennsylvania, ECE was a "weak institution" in each state; programs and services were scattered across departments, services were difficult to access, and often ECE programs had to adhere to duplicative sets of standards (Gomez, 2014). Since consolidation, the strength of ECE in Massachusetts and Pennsylvania has increased, in part, because of the accordance of greater authority to the governance entities over policymaking. Authority is necessary for enacting and sustaining a boundary-spanning policy regime, given that it is difficult to foster integrative policies without the formalized power to do so. The EEC and OCDEL have the authority to foster integrative policies, and focus on the system rather than on individual programs.

Scope as a Regime Characteristic. Another important characteristic of a boundary-spanning policy regime is scope—both vertical and horizontal.

Vertical scope differs in Pennsylvania and Massachusetts. In Massachusetts, the vertical scope of the EEC is strictly birth through kindergarten entry. Although the commissioner of the EEC collaborates closely with the commissioner of the Department of Elementary and Secondary Education, the EEC does not have jurisdictional authority for children kindergarten through grade 3. The EEC, in essence, is dependent on the staff in the Department of Elementary and Secondary Education to either grant permissive authority to the EEC, or to collaborate with the department to work on policies related to kindergarten through grade 3.

In Pennsylvania, the limit of the vertical scope is grade 3, but within the K–3 age range there is a narrower horizontal scope. That is to say that, while OCDEL's authority extends through grade 3, the policies, programs, and services related to grades 1–3 that it oversees are limited.

The decision to create an office with oversight provided by both Education and Welfare in Pennsylvania is inherently related to scope. With authority over a portion of the K–12 system, OCDEL doesn't have to try to get buy-in from the K–12 system in the same way that the EEC does; rather, it has at least some degree of authority over the K–3 segment of the K–12 system and, thus, some decisionmaking power. The vertical boundary here, then, is more permeable than it might be in Massachusetts.

Horizontally, the scope of consolidated governance in Massachusetts and Pennsylvania is similar for programs targeting children birth through kindergarten entry. Horizontal scope is defined as the number, or breadth, of programs and services that are included in an office's purview. It is a construct that helps clarify the degree to which consolidated governance has mitigated fragmentation by moving resources. Table 3.1 includes a list of programs and services provided by the EEC and OCDEL.

In Pennsylvania, the goal was to bring together the expertise and the resources to support early childhood into one office to create a continuum of services and centralize policymaking. This meant combining the resources from welfare and education to maximize resources—both financial and human. The goal of maximizing resources is an example of the allocation functions of consolidated governance that were articulated above.

OCDEL's centralized policymaking provides further evidence that consolidated approaches to governance rise to the level of a BSPR. Joachim and May (2010) posit that boundary-spanning policy regimes have the ability to "reduce policy fragmentation with respect to a particular messy problem" (p. 317). The idea that policymaking is centralized in OCDEL and that the array of ECE programs in the commonwealth fall under that centralized approach to policymaking further suggests that OCDEL would meet the criteria for a boundary-spanning policy regime.

Table 3.1. Programs and Services Subsumed Under Consolidated Entities in Pennsylvania and Massachusetts: Horizontal Scope

Operational Element	OCDEL[1]	EEC[2]
Regulatory	Certification Services	Licensing
Subsidy and Assistance in Locating Child Care	Child-Care Works (i.e., subsidy, assistance to parents in finding ECE programs)	Financial Assistance for Families Find Early Education & Care Programs
Family Support and Engagement	Children's Trust Fund (i.e., family support) Nurse-Family Partnership and Parent-Child Home Program (i.e., family support)	Parent Engagement and Family Support
Improve Program Quality	Keystone Babies Keystone STARS (i.e., QRIS) Pennsylvania Pre-K Counts Head Start Supplemental, OCDEL Early Head Start Grant	Provider and Program Administration (i.e., QRIS, Head Start)
Early Intervention/ IDEA	Early Intervention, including IDEA parts B and C	IDEA parts B and C
Workforce Supports	Public-Private Partnerships (i.e., grants to agencies to provide support services, including professional development)	Workforce and Professional Development Curriculum and Learning Funding Opportunities

1. Office of Child Development and Learning Annual Report (OCDEL, 2012)

2. Massachusetts Department of Early Education and Care website (2013) retrieved from www.mass.gov/edu/government/departments-and-boards/department-of-early-education-and-care/

The reduction of policy fragmentation in the Massachusetts ECE system has also occurred as a result of the creation of the EEC. A strategic planning document developed by the EEC notes that the state aimed not simply to consolidate existing programs, merge departments or simplify organizational charts. Instead, EEC was born from a top-to-bottom rethinking of how to orient state resources to support families in ways that are responsive to their needs. The scope is broad and presents an opportunity for sweeping statewide impact, dramatically improving the quality and affordability of programs, and expanding access to hundreds of thousands of children and their families. (Department of Early Education and Care, 2009, p. 4)

As this quote illustrates, a philosophical "reorientation" of resources was the solution to the policy problems outlined in the subsection on states' rationales for choice of form. In other words, the EEC was designed to be an elegant solution to a "particular messy problem." The EEC also centralized policymaking for ECE for programs and services, including Universal Pre-K, Head Start, licensing, child-care subsidy, the state's QRIS, and professional development for the ECE workforce. Thus, its scope is horizontally as broad as OCDEL's.

THE ADVANTAGE OF CONSOLIDATED APPROACHES FOR GOVERNING COMPLEX ADAPTIVE SYSTEMS: HIGH ADAPTIVE CAPACITY

Adaptive capacity is the ability of a particular governance approach to respond to changes (occurring both within the ECE system it governs and the wider political, cultural, and economic environments in which it operates), and to make adjustments in its governance strategies based on these changes for the purpose of effectively managing the system. Because complex adaptive systems have behavior that is difficult to predict, a high adaptive capacity is a critical aspect of effective governance of a CAS.

In conceptualizing the adaptive capacities of the EEC and OCDEL, I borrow from Duit and Galaz's (2008) typology of governance, in which they define adaptive capacity according to the concepts of *exploration* and *exploitation*. Exploration is the capacity of a governance approach to be creative, to innovate, and to experiment. In essence, exploration is the ability to be flexible and to explore a variety of strategies for governing complex systems. Exploitation is the capacity of a governance approach to leverage new and existing resources and integrate them into the system with efficiency (Duit & Galaz, 2008).

Duit and Galaz (2008) articulate four types of adaptive capacity: fragile, flexible, rigid, and robust. Governance approaches that are fragile have low capacities for exploration and exploitation. Governance approaches that are highly flexible are better able to explore new resources and strategies for governing complex systems and, therefore, have high exploratory capacities. These approaches, however, do not have the power to implement effectively and, as a result, are not able to fully exploit the results of their exploration. Rigid governance approaches, on the other hand, are highly powerful and have the ability to exploit resources and ideas for their benefit, but have low capacities for exploration. As such, their governance strategies are constrained by a lack of innovation. Robust capacities are both highly flexible and highly powerful, thus rendering a high adaptive capacity with the ability to explore and exploit resources.

The data I collected on OCDEL and the EEC suggest that consolidated approaches to governance have robust adaptive capacities. The challenge, particularly for governing complex adaptive systems, is developing a balance of both exploration (flexibility) and exploitation (power). The robust adaptive capacity of consolidated governance stems from the eight functions of governance found in Massachusetts and Pennsylvania, discussed earlier, which have particular relevance for thinking about the ability of a governance entity to both *effect* and *respond to* change. These functions can be categorized as either exploratory or exploitative.

Exploratory Functions

Planning, collaboration, outreach and engagement, and quality functions have primarily exploratory aims. These functions enable consolidated governance entities in the focal states to innovate, to experiment with different operational and philosophical models, and to take risks (Duit & Galaz, 2008). One example of exploration is the EEC's success in planning and executing its successful application for the Race to the Top–Early Learning Challenge Grant. The EEC used its allocation and planning functions to effectively explore (i.e., seek new resources). Notably, an individual involved in writing the state's application said that the EEC's high degree of authority and consolidated structure allowed for the application committee to write the grant unencumbered by the logistical concerns that plagued other states, such as trying to determine which state agency would be the lead for administering the funds.

Exploitative Functions

The governance functions of allocation, accountability, standard-setting, and regulation represent exploitative functions. These functions enable the consolidated entities to be productive, to implement programs and services with consistency, and to monitor their work for the purposes of increasing efficiency and effectiveness. Examples of these functions, as carried out by OCDEL and the EEC, are illustrative of a high exploitative capacity. For instance, OCDEL uses its integrated data system (called PELICAN—Pennsylvania's Enterprise to Link Information for Children Across Networks) to assess needs, and then it quickly reallocates resources to where in the ECE system the resources are most needed. This exploitative capacity means that the commonwealth can make data-driven decisions when responding to changes in the ECE system.

Historical Perspective

Consolidated governance approaches in the focal states are, in part, robust because of the range of functions available to them. It is perhaps useful to contrast the examples of exploration and exploitation provided here with the fragmented approaches to ECE governance that have historically existed in the United States, or even what existed in Massachusetts and Pennsylvania prior to consolidation.

Arguably, consolidation has moved Massachusetts and Pennsylvania from governance approaches with lower adaptive capacity to a higher adaptive capacity. Before consolidation, the extant policy problems indicated that governance in these states was fragile in nature. Both states suffered from a lack of communication between ECE programs and the administrative structures to which they were held accountable, little formal coordination across programmatic and fiscal silos, an unstable workforce, and low levels of ECE program quality (Gomez, 2014). Massachusetts and Pennsylvania also exhibited rigid characteristics of governance prior to consolidation, including duplicative sets of regulations, standards, and funding streams to which ECE programs were required to adhere. The administrative entities had the power to implement these standards, but not necessarily the authority to explore across departments' methods of reducing duplication.

IMPLICATIONS AND CONCLUSIONS

The goal of this chapter was to share a set of findings from a qualitative study of two states with consolidated approaches to governance, as a mechanism through which to conceptualize the relative capacities of consolidated approaches to governance for bringing coherence to state ECE systems.

These findings suggest that consolidation can render powerful structures with broad scopes of service, defined here as boundary-spanning policy regimes. As BSPRs, regardless of form, the EEC and OCDEL carry out a set of common functions. These functions can be categorized as exploitative or exploratory and yield a robust adaptive capacity to govern. I have argued that robustness is important in a governance approach because it enables both a powerful and flexible response to changes within the ECE system, as well as to exogenous economic or political changes. This ability to adapt is an asset (if not a necessity) for the governance of ECE systems because ECE systems are complex adaptive systems and, thus, are notoriously difficult to manage.

More data on governance generally and consolidated approaches to governance specifically are most certainly needed, but these findings illustrate that there are important lessons from research that have long been neglected in examining ECE governance. Conceptualizing ECE governance within the frame of complex adaptive systems theory will hopefully set the stage for more utilitarian and effective governance designs. This analysis also empirically revealed what has been tacitly acknowledged in practice: that one governance *form* may not fit all states, but that there are transcendent *functions* attendant to effective approaches to governance, and that governance functionality may have implications for the *durability* of a governance entity. Finally, I hope that this chapter will shed both practical and theoretical light as the field establishes governance entities as the central force in both system development and more efficient delivery of services for young children and their families.

NOTE

1. The study on which this chapter is based also included Delaware as a sample state. At the time of this writing, however, Delaware had not yet decided whether it was going to adopt a consolidated approach to governance so findings related to this state were not included.

REFERENCES

Department of Early Education and Care (EEC). (2009). Department of early education and care strategic plan: Putting children and families first. Retrieved from www.mass.gov/Eeoe/docs/EEC/fy09_legis_rpt/5yr_strategic_plan.pdf
Department of Early Education and Care (EEC). (2013). *Programs and services provided by the Department*. Retrieved from www.mass.gov/edu/government/departments-and-boards/department-of-early-education-and-care

Duit, A., & Galaz, V. (2008). Governance and complexity—Emerging issues for governance theory. *Governance: An International Journal of Policy, Administration, and Institutions, 21*(3), 311–335.

Goffin, S. E., Martella, J., & Coffman, J. (2011). *Vision to practice: Setting a new course for early childhood governance.* Washington, DC: Goffin Strategy Group.

Gomez, R. E. (2014). *Exploring the potential of consolidated approaches to governance for bringing coherence to early childhood systems.* (Doctoral dissertation). Retrieved from ProQuest Dissertations and Theses. (UMI 3621772)

Gomez, R. E., Kagan, S. L., & Khanna, S. (2012). *Selecting an approach to governance: Choices related to form, function, and durability.* New York, NY: National Center for Children and Families.

Joachim, A., & May, J. R. (2010). Beyond subsystems: Policy regimes and governance. *Policy Studies Journal 38*(2), 303–327.

Kagan, S. L., & Cohen, N. E. (1997). *Not by chance: Creating an early care and education system.* New Haven, CT: Yale University Bush Center in Child Development and Social Policy.

Kagan, S. L., & Kauerz, K. (2008). Governing American early care and education: Shifting from government to governance and from form to function. In S. Feeney, A. Galper, & C. Seefeldt (Eds.), *Continuing issues in early childhood education* (3rd ed.) (pp. 12–32). Columbus, OH: Pearson Merrill Prentice Hall.

Kauerz, K., & Kagan, S. L. (2012). Governance and early childhood systems: Different forms, similar goals. In S. L. Kagan & K. Kauerz (Eds.), *Early childhood systems: Transforming early learning* (pp. 87–103). New York, NY: Teachers College Press.

Office of Child Development and Early Learning (OCDEL). (2012). *Pennsylvania Office of Child Development and Early Learning: 2010–2011 annual report.* Harrisburg, PA: Department of Public Welfare.

Snyder, S. (2013). The simple, the complicated, the complex: Education reform through the lens of complexity theory. *OECD Education Working Papers, No. 96.* Paris, France: OECD Publishing.

CHAPTER 4

Governance as a Driver for Systems Development

Issues of Scope and Implementation

Harriet Dichter

I first started thinking about governance of early learning systems as a strategy for improving child outcomes while working with a community coalition whose focus was on building a quality system at the state level that would serve our large, urban community well. Our coalition consisted of policy advocates, communications specialists, professional development and technical assistance leaders, and early childhood directors and teachers. I was initially unsure of the priority we should place on governance as a means to effect change. How would governance relate to improved outcomes—would we be able to show sufficient concrete outcomes related to children's learning? Were the issues around authority and accountability for early childhood really so problematic that tackling governance was essential? The current approach involved various state agencies, and many program offices within them, so that early learning was fragmented. To make early childhood care more effective, I felt it had to be positioned as a key educational and economic development issue with a "quality" framework, rather than a "work support" framework.

This chapter details my experiences with developing an approach to governance for early learning in Pennsylvania, and uses insights gained in the process to reflect more broadly on the importance of consolidated approaches to governance for the functioning of state early learning systems.

CASE STUDY: PENNSYLVANIA'S OFFICE
OF CHILD DEVELOPMENT AND EARLY LEARNING

Moving from a position of community leadership to public service at the state level during Governor Ed Rendell's term provided me with an inside opportunity to tackle governance and to test the value of a new governance approach as one of many reform and transformation strategies for early childhood.

Phase One: Creation of the Office

Working for Governor Ed Rendell, I started with appointments in both the Education and Public Welfare departments: as policy director in Education, where we were starting new early childhood programs, and at the same time, as the founding deputy secretary for child development at Public Welfare, where we brought together for the first time the early childhood programs that were scattered throughout the child welfare, income security, and developmental disabilities offices of the agency.

This first phase of consolidating governance within the Public Welfare agency took place over a 3-month period in 2004, and it had terrific support and interest both inside state government and with key stakeholders from around the state. Within state government, the strategy of consolidation placed a higher priority on the early learning programs by elevating them to their own office (the Office of Child Development and Early Learning), equal to the other key offices within each state agency. The staff that moved into the new office saw the opportunity and value-add for leveraging expertise, breaking down silos, and better serving children and families. Stakeholders were also enthusiastic about having a single home for the early childhood programs housed in the Public Welfare agency. This initial consolidation within the Public Welfare agency into one brand-new program office brought together child-care licensing, birth-to-3 early intervention, child-care assistance, and child-care quality initiatives, including the professional development system, as well as the newly developing Quality Rating and Improvement System (QRIS). The office had responsibility for program and policy development, implementation, data systems, resource development, and budget and fiscal matters, premised on core values of equity and quality.

At the same time, we were developing new initiatives and seeking to build an educational framework for the programming through new work at the Department of Education and through cross-cutting work that involved both Education and Public Welfare. For example, within the Department of Education, we introduced financing to stimulate full-day kindergarten, and we created a Head Start Supplemental.

Phase Two: Implementation and Expansion

Although we were making progress by consolidating all of the work in support of early learning in the Public Welfare agency into one office, we were squarely connecting early learning to educational outcomes through the new startups occurring at the Education agency, and we had one accountable appointed official (through my joint appointment as policy director in Education and as deputy secretary in Public Welfare), so we still had two big silos.

The arrangement had many benefits, but it was not without its problems. We needed greater staff capacity and expertise in both agencies (e.g., policy development, program implementation, finance, and IT) and to be more efficient with the staff we had. We had startup program efforts in two state agencies, although they focused on the needs of the same children. We were running early education programs out of the policy office, which was designed to focus on policy and not on operations, which was not sustainable over time. It was hard to focus on breaking down silos to help move the work forward.

In response to these challenges, we created one unified office, the Office of Child Development and Early Learning (OCDEL), in 2006. OCDEL was designed to serve as the lead for all of the state's early learning programs, whether they originated within the Public Welfare or within the Education agency. In contrast to other states, such as North Carolina or Maryland, which had transferred all funding, program responsibility, and staff to one state agency, we found a way to create one office with singular responsibility for funding, program, and staff, but under the auspices of two agencies. The new office was created to have an identical existence on the organizational chart of the two agencies contributing the resources—Education and the Public Welfare (Human Services) agency—with a director (called the deputy secretary) appointed by the governor and authorized through an order of the Pennsylvania Executive Board. This new organization brought together the work associated with the original consolidation at Public Welfare, along with new initiatives tied to appropriations for Education, such as pre-K, as well as the existing Part B preschool Early Intervention program. The organization has proven itself to be sufficiently flexible during and responsive to transition into new gubernatorial leadership and a second generation of leadership staff.

THINKING ABOUT ECE GOVERNANCE EFFORTS

Although Pennsylvania used consolidation as its governance strategy, it did so in a unique manner; many years later, the Pennsylvania governance strategy has been sustained, but it still remains a unique variant, appropriate to the state context. Other states have chosen different solutions within the overall strategy of consolidation—creating new early childhood–only agencies (e.g., the Department of Early Learning in Washington or Georgia) or consolidating their work into either the education (e.g., Maryland) or human services (e.g., North Carolina) agency.

These approaches are unified by a common drive to use governance to maximize benefits across the variety of essential stakeholders: children and families served; "backbone" or "infrastructure" organizations that are essential to success; programs, teachers, and administrators who work with young children and their families; and advocates and policymakers. At the same time, these unifying governance models also value and implement an approach in which they emphasize the traditional values of efficiency and prudency in government. These models reflect commonly agreed-upon core values in governance, including alignment in areas critical to children's outcomes and essential to efficient governance, such as screening and assessments, early learning standards, and data collection; accountability, both external to the early childhood system and its stakeholders and internal, through supporting strong accountability for the services which it invests in and sponsors; and sustainability that permits the governance model to work within an evolving state political and policy context (Regenstein & Lipper, 2013).

IMPLEMENTING TRANSFORMATIVE GOVERNANCE

Although perhaps less commonly stated, integration is another core value that we see in the consolidation governance strategies. In Pennsylvania, OCDEL brought together all of the early childhood policy, resources, and program development and implementation, thus even further enabling the acceleration of change. New efforts were conceptualized in an interdependent and integrated manner. For example, when Pennsylvania was able to launch its pre-K program, it built on the Quality Rating and Improvement System, by requiring child-care programs to achieve a specified QRIS level, and by leveraging the technical assistance, monitoring, and professional development systems that were already in place to support a focus on quality early learning and school readiness. A unified governance structure provided the opportunity to insist on alignment *and* integration across programs.

The high-level concepts that those inside early childhood cite as the case for unified governance (i.e., alignment, accountability, efficiency, integration, and sustainability) are one part of making the case for unified governance. But these high-level arguments do not work for everyone. Transformative governance requires buy-in from many people who are not close to the day-to-day work of early childhood care. These people include government officials, families, agency and program leaders, and providers. Quality and consistency are also important to transformative governance.

The Need for Buy-In

Practical reasons and illustrations are often necessary to create buy-in for implementing a consolidated approach to governance. The same reasons may not apply in all situations and state-specific illustrations are critical for making arguments persuasive. Making the case for consolidated governance as a practical and effective way of improving outcomes for children and for creating an equitable approach to early learning and its financing, programming, and services, requires vision, courage, and concrete examples.

Many senior appointees in the Pennsylvania executive branch had to agree to the work, and buy-in is also needed in those states that involve not only executive branch leadership but also the legislative branch. Neither elected nor appointed public officials want to use their limited time and resources to press forward on governance unless they believe it will make a concrete and meaningful difference in the early learning mission, which typically involves a focus on improved outcomes for young children, particularly those who are at great risk and who have significant needs. Changing from a fragmented to a unified governance approach can sound a lot like spending time and potentially money in favor of bureaucracy or kingdom-building, rather than in favor of transformative change that benefits young children, their families, and the professionals who work with them.

Consolidation (in Pennsylvania and in other states) has resulted in a unified message and in a one-stop shop for early learning in these states, bringing together all the information about the state's early learning options. In most states, multiple agencies are communicating via written, electronic, and face-to-face information. The information is often limited to the perspective of the agency/organization that is communicating. This means that families are missing out or are being forced to go to multiple entities to get the information that they need. Consolidated governance puts the focus on ensuring consistency.

In early childhood programs, leaders have multiple roles, often serving as instructional, family, and administrative leaders for their programs. Early childhood program leaders are spending time dealing with mixed and/or conflicting messages from the various state agencies—time that could be better spent supporting quality instruction and family engagement, and creating the world-class early learning system that we envision for children and their families. A consolidated structure helps free up time for this more critical work. Leaders in these programs have more time to spend on the programs being offered to children—that is, teaching and learning. They also have more time to spend on parent-family partnerships and less time on bureaucracy, thus supporting improved quality services for children and families.

Furthermore, early childhood programs are often visited, monitored, and provided technical assistance by multiple state agencies. This may not only be inconvenient for the individuals working in these programs, but it can also lead to inconsistent priorities, communications, and supports from the various agencies. In attempting to meet various requirements, program leaders must work with more than one agency on similar issues, sometimes leading to conflicting results. Consolidated governance can spur a more efficient multidisciplinary team that could combine visits, have consistent messages for providers, help prioritize needed improvements and supports, and determine the proper scope of any monitoring that takes place in order to avoid duplication. Programs also benefit from having government entities working together to determine areas that are in need of support and how to address those areas with existing resources, rather than acting at cross-purposes, as is so often the case when there are multiple agencies setting requirements for ECE programs.

Individuals working in ECE programs also benefit from consistent messaging/feedback regarding the areas in which they are doing well, areas of challenge, and services available to address those areas. Consolidated governance gives providers an opportunity to receive consistent feedback that is particularly important when the support they need is for the critical area of quality improvement. Having consolidated governance can also help avoid situations where providers feel that one program is affirming that they are doing well, but another state agency and program has evidence of less than acceptable performance. Likewise, a consolidated approach puts the state in a better place to make sure that exemplary ECE programs and their employees are more consistently promoted and supported in their work.

Quality and Consistency

As illustrated in the Pennsylvania case study, consolidated governance promotes consistent policies and priorities, which has implications for the entire system. Here, I look at the implications for three segments of the ECE system: ECE program quality, workforce supports and staff qualifications, and data management and accountability functions.

The concepts that are important to ECE program quality should be reinforced consistently across the ECE system to enable more rapid improvements. For example, are the early learning standards meaningfully promoted and implemented across all the state's early childhood programs? Are they implemented across different types of ECE programs (e.g., publicly funded pre-K, Head Start, nonprofit and for-profit child care)? Providing a consolidated approach to governance puts a higher premium on consistent promotion, implementation support, and follow-through.

ECE professionals frequently contend with different professional credentialing and development requirements related to various state programs. Consolidated governance highlights these discrepancies and pushes the state to focus on the human capital needs of its teachers and leaders. For example, moving toward a consolidated approach to governance in Pennsylvania has resulted in a comprehensive career lattice for the ECE profession and an array of programmatic and financial supports to help professionals achieve higher levels on that lattice. In addition, a consolidated approach enabled the commonwealth to develop quality assurance mechanisms for professional development and technical assistance that ensure that these supports are of high quality and that they are implemented with consistency across sectors and across the commonwealth.

In many states, the different agencies involved in early childhood work all use their own data systems, and this creates several problems. First, systems are typically narrow, designed to serve the immediate program need without consideration of the whole program. Second, the data systems are not interoperable and do not communicate with one another, exacerbating efforts to look at program data as a whole. Third, although most states now have a goal of obtaining a longitudinal data system for early childhood, the typical narrow focus and lack of coherent, high-level executive leadership for an integrated data system cause additional problems. Consolidated governance can enable consideration and action on all of these issues, and can provide more appropriate executive sponsorship and opportunity for action.

CONCLUSIONS

The drive to improve outcomes for young children, both in the short and long term, is the most powerful reason to think about early childhood governance as a strategy for change. Although the particular points that help persuade decisionmakers to go forward with a new governance approach will vary from state to state, a critical part of the case is demonstrating the connection between governance and improvements for young children and their families. Tangible improvements can occur, and, through consolidated governance, the system and the many stakeholders it serves derive several benefits, including:

- Improved coordination, alignment, and communication by having multiple programs under one roof
- Collaboration and energy around a common purpose
- More holistic development of policies
- Information sharing and planning regarding work with individual providers that will help consistently embed safety and quality into their programs
- Improved accountability with one governance authority versus separate silos
- Higher-level positions within early childhood, making it easier to attract top talent
- Increased visibility of the issues through better positioning of early learning in the overall state organization of services and resources
- Improved customer service for consumers—families and providers—who are confused by multiple names and organizational homes and separate processes for services
- Creation of a common professional development platform and a common monitoring and technical assistance platform, driven by the same values, standards, and expectations for children's outcomes

These benefits outweigh the costs and challenges of developing and implementing a consolidated approach to governance. Governance is a reform that states may wish to consider as they think about their services for young children and families, and when they think about the ECE field itself.

REFERENCE

Regenstein, E., & Lipper, K. (2013). *A framework for choosing a state level governance system.* BUILD Initiative. Retrieved from http://www.buildinitiative. org/Portals/0/Uploads/Documents/Early%20Childhood%20Governance%20 for%20Web.pdf

Part III

GOVERNANCE AND SYSTEMS DEVELOPMENT

CHAPTER 5

The Intersection of Quality Rating and Improvement Systems and ECE Governance

Kate Tarrant and Diana Schaack

The lack of coherence within and across sectors of the early care and education system has raised concerns about inequitable access to high-quality programs for children and families and has contributed to disparities in young children's developmental outcomes (General Accounting Office, 2000; Kagan, 2006). Historically, early childhood education (ECE) has been administered by numerous agencies, provided through disparate organizations, and studied through a variety of disciplines. Consequently, ECE planners and practitioners confront a legacy of fragmentation. In response, there is a proliferation of efforts to unify the ECE field to provide young children and their families with cohesive, equitable, and responsive services that bolster opportunities for lifelong success. This chapter explores two complementary strategies that have significant implications for the coherence of the ECE field: governance and Quality Rating and Improvement Systems (QRIS). As priorities in the federal government's 2010 and 2013 Race to the Top–Early Learning Challenge grant competitions, governance and QRIS are at the forefront of most states' early care and education policy agenda; thus, the relationship between these complementary strategies warrants discussion. In this chapter, we argue that these strategies can work in tandem to move the ECE system forward in delivering seamless access to excellent services for children and families.

This chapter unpacks the relationship between QRIS and ECE governance structures to describe the ways in which QRIS may theoretically impact the overall ECE system and how greater attention to governance may strengthen QRIS. It begins with a historical review of quality rating and improvement systems, and then explains the evolution of QRIS from a child-care improvement intervention to a potential policy strategy to build a more cohesive ECE system. We then introduce two key aspects of well-functioning early childhood governance structures—accountability and authority—and discuss the relationship between governance and QRIS with examples from states. The chapter concludes with a discussion of a framework for analyzing QRIS governance.

QRIS: HISTORY AND EVOLUTION

QRIS emerged in the late 1990s as a multifaceted intervention, primarily directed at community-based child-care programs, to strengthen the quality of care available to children and families. QRIS establish common center and family child-care program quality standards that are organized into levels of rigor and then utilize a multidimensional assessment of program, classroom, and practitioner quality to assign star ratings to programs based on their compliance with these standards. QRIS standards typically address the classroom learning environment, staff qualifications, family involvement, and classroom ratios, and frequently include leadership and business practices and the utilization of curricula and child assessments (Tout et al., 2010). Within most states' QRIS, the first tier of the rating represents programs that comply with or modestly exceed the standards set forth by state child-care licensing standards that are aimed at protecting children's health and safety. Higher QRIS ratings reflect increasingly better levels of quality, above and beyond licensing standards. Ratings are typically used to guide program supports, such as coaching or financial incentives, which encourage programs to improve their services. In some states, ratings are made public to assist families in selecting higher-quality care for their children.

These strategies were originally conceived by a need to address a major factor underlying poor program quality in the child-care sector of the ECE industry: market failure (Helburn & Bergmann, 2002). In efficient markets, purchasers act in their own interests to select the products or services that best meet their needs and price is typically a valid indicator of quality. Furthermore, in efficient markets consumers have access to information to evaluate product quality, which fuels demand for high-quality, affordable products. In contrast, child care is characterized by market failure for numerous reasons. First, families lack adequate information to differentiate quality. Second, families' demand for excellent ECE is low, which limits the availability of care that promotes children's development and benefits society (Blau, 2011). Third, families may be unable to pay the high price for quality care. Lastly, families' willingness to pay for quality care does not account for the social benefits of high-quality care. Weak consumer demand has a ripple effect on the supply side of the child-care market and limits the availability of excellent care. Because families do not demand quality care, the cost of improved program quality typically falls on the shoulders of an underpaid workforce, fueling high teacher turnover, which further suppresses program quality (Whitebook, Howes, & Phillips, 1990). Within a context of scarce resources, programs either compromise quality or increase parent tuition, which can have the adverse consequence of funneling families and their children into unregulated and, frequently, lower-quality care (Helburn & Bergmann, 2002).

Mitchell (2005) and Stoney (2004) suggest that QRIS may intervene on both the supply and demand sides of the child-care market to improve the availability of high-quality services. To address the supply-side problem, QRIS provide an accountability tool (e.g., the star ratings) so that government and other agencies may direct funding toward programs that have higher ratings (Stoney, 2004), thereby encouraging programs to offer higher-quality care. In addition, QRIS may assist in legitimizing government investment in ECE that can be measured by star rating increases. Thus, star ratings may help garner additional public and private funding that can be targeted toward quality improvement interventions that can increase the number of high-quality programs in a state.

To address the demand-side problem, quality ratings may serve as an education tool so consumers (i.e., families, governments, and foundations) can make informed decisions about where to spend their ECE dollars (Mitchell, 2009; Stoney, 2004). Policymakers may also further enhance demand by using ratings to direct funding toward families who select higher-quality programs in the form of tax credits or differential tuition credits. In theory, the supply- and demand-side interventions may ameliorate child-care market inefficiencies and result in higher-quality care and better developmental outcomes for young children.

Although QRIS are primarily seen as a program-level quality improvement strategy or market intervention, there is growing recognition that they are also a mechanism to strengthen the cohesiveness of a state's overall ECE system (Mitchell, 2009). Indeed, some states are redesigning or building QRIS with an eye toward aligning program standards and coordinating quality improvement strategies within and among sectors of the early childhood industry (Schaack, Tarrant, Boller, & Tout, 2012). For example, many states' QRIS extend beyond rating programs within the child-care sector and include Head Start as well as school-based prekindergarten programs. States also link QRIS with other system components such as licensing standards, professional credentialing systems, and higher education.

Although QRIS objectives have expanded to include ECE system-building, the relationship between ECE governance structures and QRIS—including its efficacy as an accountability tool within the ECE system and its authority regarding setting standards, managing resources, and implementing QRIS activities—does not appear to be integral to many state QRIS designs. We contend that the nature of a state's ECE governance structure influences the tools that a QRIS mobilizes to improve program quality and bring accountability to the system.

QRIS AND GOVERNANCE

We set the stage for our discussion with Kauerz and Kagan's (2012) definition of governance: "governance includes the structures, processes, and policies that enable a system to function consistently, effectively, and efficiently" (p. 88). They add that good governance addresses both accountability and authority (Kagan & Kauerz, 2008; Kauerz & Kagan, 2012). These two constructs are instrumental to any understanding of QRIS' potential as a system-builder. QRIS are one of the ECE system's prevalent accountability structures whose impact, we contend, hinges on the authority with which each QRIS is imbued.

Accountability: QRIS as a Governance Tool for the ECE System

One of QRIS' lauded features is that it has the potential to serve as a system-wide accountability strategy, a process by which programs may be rewarded or sanctioned based on their performance. In the education sector, accountability systems typically follow a four-stage process: (1) standards development, (2) assessment, (3) data collection, and (4) program improvement (Schultz, 2010). As QRIS evolved to address child-care market inefficiencies and the overall quality of participating ECE programs, their design in most states adopted this accountability framework. As discussed earlier, QRIS first establish program standards that are structured in tiers. Second, QRIS establish assessment procedures to monitor programs' compliance with the standards through a combination of documentation reviews and classroom or program observations. Third, QRIS facilitate data collection and reporting. Finally, assessment data are analyzed and often used for data-driven quality improvement, which incorporates numerous strategies: financial assistance, professional development, coaching, and technical assistance. Although QRIS are an ECE program accountability tool, there are two issues with their influence within the ECE system: (1) cross-state variation in QRIS design and (2) QRIS coordination among accountability systems.

Cross-State Variation in QRIS Design. First, QRIS do not provide a consistent perspective on the performance of ECE programs writ large because QRIS design and implementation vary tremendously across states (Tout et al., 2010). QRIS program standards differ in their complexity based on the number of standards, the organization of the standards, and the scoring of the standards. Assessment and ongoing monitoring procedures range in rigor, with some states conducting observational assessments of all programs and other states relying primarily on self-reports from participating programs. In addition, the majority of states collect observational assessments on a sample of classrooms within a center, while others (e.g., Colorado) collect observations on all classrooms. As a result, a star rating does not carry the same meaning across states or even across communities within a given state (e.g., California).

States also vary with respect to their data management. Data management can be coherent, with data easily accessed and housed within one entity in states that have a well-developed data infrastructure, or data collection may be idiosyncratic, with program-, classroom-, and teacher-level data housed in a number of entities, creating data access and reporting difficulties. Further, the dissemination of results is not uniform: Some states have invested in media campaigns to publicize ratings to influence family's ECE decisions (e.g., Minnesota) while other states have kept the ratings primarily internal until they have a critical mass of program participation (e.g., New York). In addition, investments in improvement are highly variable in intensity and design (Tout et al., 2010). Finally, the density and scale of QRIS participation differs wildly across states. This variation, which is expected because QRIS are a state-level policy mechanism, suggests that QRIS may be well-functioning accountability tools in some states but not in others.

With QRIS now moving into their second decade, research is emerging on QRIS design issues that may help bring uniformity to many QRIS, including cut-scores on quality measures within a QRIS related to better child outcomes that can be used to derive a star rating (Le, Schaack, & Setodji, in press), the reliability of data collection decisions (Karoly, Zellman, & Perlman, 2013), and the effectiveness of specific quality improvement approaches (Boller, Blair, Del Grosso, & Paulsell, 2010). Furthermore, with the implementation of Race to the Top–Early Learning Challenge Grants, at least 15 states are in the process of conducting validation studies of their QRIS; they are studying associations between ratings levels and child outcomes and examining the efficacy of their quality improvement strategies. These data hold incredible potential for future meta-analyses that may help identify QRIS standards related to better teaching and learning outcomes, determine reliable data collection methods, and create an evidence base for quality improvement approaches. QRIS validation research may also help streamline the assessment component of QRIS across states, reduce the cost of implementation efforts, and allow for more funding to be directed toward evidence-based improvement efforts. Such research may help garner greater consensus on QRIS' accountability features—program standards, assessment, data reporting, and quality improvement—that is needed to strengthen their potential to ensure young children receive excellent care.

QRIS Coordination Among Accountability Systems. The second issue with the functionality of QRIS as an accountability framework for the ECE system is that QRIS are one among many accountability tools that are used in the early care and education context (National Early Childhood Accountability Task Force, 2007). Each major early childhood funding stream—Head Start, CCDF, IDEA, and state-funded prekindergarten—has its own program and practitioner accountability systems.

To start, there are several accountability structures within the child-care sector. State licensing is the accountability structure that guides community-based family child-care homes and centers. Licensing regulations focus on program-level standards that emphasize safety and health and set minimal levels of educational requirements to obtain different teaching positions. Designed to raise the bar above licensing standards in community-based programs, national accreditation systems, such as the National Association for the Education for Young Children and the National Association for Family Child Care, set program standards and practitioner educational standards. In addition, the ECE system in many states also includes either voluntary or mandatory ECE teacher credentialing structures, which are sometimes connected to the state's QRIS.

Other sectors of the ECE industry have different accountability demands, many of which involve evaluations of teaching quality and assessments of children's learning. It is important to note, however, that there is a distinction between requirements to use child assessments as part of an accountability system and using child assessments as outcomes to reward or sanction programs. Because of the instability of children's learning and development during early childhood (Meisels & Atkins-Burnett, 2006), child assessment outcomes are not used as an accountability measure the way they are used in K–12 settings.

For instance, Head Start holds programs accountable by monitoring compliance with its lengthy performance standards that span service delivery related to promoting children's health, family well-being, and children's learning. Head Start accountability and monitoring systems require programs to use child assessments to inform teaching, curricular decisions, and services. These service delivery standards are broader and deeper in scope than standards set forth within QRIS. Similarly, some public school–based prekindergarten classrooms have accountability structures aligned with the K–12 accountability frameworks that emphasize teacher effectiveness as well as the use of child assessments.

Programs designated for children who have special needs are subject to a completely different set of standards and are largely oriented around the development and use of children's individualized education plans. For the many early childhood programs that leverage numerous funding sources, they are held accountable to numerous sets of program, teaching, and child standards, and a QRIS functions as one among many competing demands.

What makes QRIS stand out and what makes many advocates, researchers, and practitioners so excited about the potential for QRIS as a system-builder is that they are the one accountability tool that, if designed appropriately, can be uniformly applied across program types. Theoretically, QRIS can bring the many subsystems together to improve the coordination and alignment of standards, assessment, data collection, and professional development. This coordination may lead to greater efficiency within the overall systems. The impact of the QRIS in improving coherence, however, must be considered in light of the ECE system's many other accountability structures—and this is why the authority of a QRIS is so important.

Authority: Governance of the QRIS

How is a state's QRIS governed? What authority does the state's QRIS have? The degree of authority that the QRIS has to monitor programs' adherence to the standards and engage their participation has received scant attention to date. Even in the broader literature on K–12 education accountability systems, governance is rarely investigated (Brewer, Killeen, & Welsh, 2013). We suggest that greater attention to the authority of QRIS could deepen the field's understanding of QRIS' role within the broader ECE system and its potential to serve as a system-wide accountability tool. In this section, we consider QRIS authority in several ways: (1) oversight structure, (2) statutory or regulatory framework, and (3) high-stakes financial incentives.

Oversight Structure. First, the unity and power of the QRIS' oversight structure may influence QRIS funding levels as well as public perceptions of the system's legitimacy (Kagan & Kauerz, 2008). When a state agency has the sole responsibility for the oversight of the QRIS, it likely has the power to make and enforce the regulatory and funding decisions that are needed for QRIS implementation. As a result, ECE programs may be more likely to acknowledge the legitimacy of the QRIS within the broader ECE system. The authority of many states' QRIS is rarely so concentrated, however (Tout et al., 2010). Most states engage numerous partners to administer the QRIS and oversee early childhood. One unit may conduct the assessment visits while another unit provides coaching. Sometimes, states use contractors and subcontractors to fulfill these roles. Some states devolve administration authority to county-level governance structures (e.g., California). And in at least one state, Colorado, the QRIS was established in 1998 independently from the state government.

Statutory or Regulatory Framework. The second consideration is whether the QRIS is established in statute or regulation. Legal authority imbues the system with legitimacy (Weber, 1958) as well as stability. One review of states' QRIS indicates that several states have QRIS-related legislation: Kentucky, North Carolina, Rhode Island, Tennessee, and Wisconsin (National Center on Child Care Quality Improvement, 2012). Not only does statutory inclusion promote legitimacy, but legislation can also provide guidance when regulatory authorities are unable to authorize every aspect of the QRIS. For example, North Carolina's rated license is actually a property right that needs a repeal process to revoke. The legislative authority of North Carolina's system is noteworthy because the QRIS and the child-care licensing system are fully integrated so that all licensed ECE programs are rated at the lowest level of the rating system. In other words, participation in the state's QRIS is mandatory for licensed programs. Other states, such as Arkansas, Iowa, Louisiana, and Oklahoma, have administrative regulations that guide the QRIS (National Center on Child Care Quality Improvement, 2012). Regulations are enacted by the executive branch of government and have the binding effect of a law. Statutory and regulatory authority has the benefit of stability because it takes legislative action or the due process of an administrative rule change to revoke the system.

The way that the QRIS is represented in legislation, even at the sub-state level, has important implications for its authority. For example, Colorado's system is not established in state statute but one community has early childhood city-level legislation that establishes the provision of extra funding to prekindergarten programs and for tuition credits to families contingent on a QRIS rating. Such local legislation serves to increase the legitimacy of the QRIS but with legislation sun-setting, the stability of the system is uncertain.

High-Stakes Financial Incentives. A third way that the QRIS can exert authority is by offering financial rewards to participating programs to in-centivize them to adhere to the QRIS' accountability framework. The design —amount, durability, and conditions—of the financial awards can influence the types of programs that participate as well as the overall numbers of participants. Many states offer time-limited funding for quality improve-ment, such as grants for materials. One-time awards are advantageous to states with unstable or limited funding for QRIS implementation; however, they may not encourage ongoing program participation in the QRIS. States may also offer funds for quality maintenance, such as tiered subsidy reim-bursement or staff compensation bonuses to encourage programs to hire and retain highly qualified personnel (Mitchell, 2012). Whether funds are time-limited or ongoing, the amount of funding awarded to a rated program matters: It must be substantial enough to address operating costs and to en-courage participation. As Mitchell (2012) notes, the generosity of financial incentives seems to influence participation levels. Just 7% of programs par-ticipate in New Hampshire's QRIS, where participants receive a one-time award that ranges from $250 to $1000, whereas 60% of eligible programs participate in Pennsylvania's QRIS, which offers time-limited improvement grants ($300–$6,000), annual quality achievement awards ($800–$63,000), annual staff retention awards ($600–$4,000 per staff), and tiered reimburse-ment for levels 2–4 (daily add-on of $0.50–$2 per child). Although there may be other explanations for differences in uptake, such as recruitment or the administrative burden of participating in the rating process, financial incentives likely play a role.

Finally, when the receipt of state funds is contingent upon a QRIS rat-ing, participation in the QRIS is technically voluntary, but participation can have very high stakes. Several states require programs to achieve a specific rating level in order to receive funding through the child-care subsidy sys-tem, such as Oklahoma where programs have to receive a "one star plus" rating or higher to participate in the state's subsidy system (National Center on Child Care Quality Improvement, 2014). The design of QRIS financial incentives must be thoughtfully considered to encourage quality practice and convey legitimacy of the overall QRIS.

Implications of QRIS Authority. QRIS' authority has implications for its legitimacy and potential to impact the coherence of the ECE field. With a high level of authority, the QRIS has coercive mechanisms—required compliance with program standards and program funding allocations— to encourage teachers and program administrators to adopt practices that support children's school readiness. With higher levels of authority, it is likely that more programs may uphold the QRIS' definition of quality practice because they are required to do so. Coercive pressures, however, may have the adverse impact of encouraging symbolic compliance with program standards that may undermine true quality improvements that may impact young children's learning (Tarrant & Huerta, in press).

When QRIS are imbued with higher levels of authority, other ancillary organizations, such as higher education and professional development organizations, may adapt their work to align with the QRIS, creating more coherence in the system. Similarly, with such authority, coordination among different sectors of ECE, with respect to differing standards, assessments, and the delivery of professional development and quality improvement supports, may become more streamlined, creating a more efficient overall system.

Alternatively, QRIS with more diffuse governance structures have less concentrated authority. Therefore, QRIS implementation that facilitates adherence to accountability standards depends on ongoing collaboration among administrative entities and the stakeholders engaging in ongoing efforts to secure buy-in. When QRIS authority is not consolidated, states may, for example, encourage participation by appealing to program staff's sense of professionalism. Such professional pressure or competition may encourage programs to engage in the reform and thus adopt new practices. This approach may have the benefit of being inclusive, but it also requires ongoing commitments from partners or the long-term viability. Indeed, there are tradeoffs inherent in alternative approaches to governing accountability systems. As Brewer and Killeen (2009), who have studied the governance of education accountability in K–12, note, "While there may be conceptual advantages for one set of arrangements over another, there is little empirical evidence that one is preferred in the sense that it leads directly to better outcomes or indirectly to more effective educational policy" (**p. 18**). Thus, to date, the mechanisms that promote adherence to standards among programs and ancillary agencies in the system are still unknown. We contend that these QRIS governance issues warrant attention and empirical investigation.

Framework for Evaluating QRIS Governance

As state policymakers consider the intersection of QRIS and governance, research investigating the implications of alternative approaches to oversight could provide important insights into QRIS design. Brewer and Smith (2008) provide one framework that can be used to benchmark the effectiveness of QRIS as an element of the overall governance structure. Their criteria for effective governance include: (1) stability, (2) accountability, (3) transparency, (4) innovation and flexibility, and (5) efficiency.

In applying this framework to QRIS, stability may be assessed in a number of ways. One factor may be the durability of the vehicles used to fund the QRIS. Funding stability would be strengthened when the QRIS is embedded in statute or other state structures that are difficult to dismantle and weaken when time-limited grant funds or private funding covering the expenses of QRIS implementation have ended. Stability is also influenced by the durability of the QRIS standards, measures, and cut-scores used to derive the rating: As the QRIS components become more common place, it is likely that organizations and ECE practitioners would comport to what is expected of them over time (Brewer, Killeen, & Welsh, 2013).

Accountability may refer to the degree to which the QRIS is evaluated based on its performance—for example, through transparent data reporting; this may include an increase in the number of programs participating in the QRIS, an increase in the number of higher-quality programs, and, as the system becomes established, an increase in the school readiness of young children. Accountability also refers to substantive oversight of the QRIS, including clear lines of authority between the different parts of the system and consequences for meeting expectations (Brewer, Killeen, & Welsh, 2013). In addition, accountability also includes a commitment to investigating the evidence regarding different QRIS design decisions.

Transparency relates to the openness of the QRIS' development and implementation. One measure of transparency could be the number and variety of stakeholders involved in designing or providing feedback on the rating process. Another indicator would be the ability of programs to clearly articulate the processes and measures by which they are evaluated. Additionally, a well-documented and accessible appeal process would increase QRIS transparency. Such transparency is likely to increase the legitimacy of the QRIS across ECE sectors.

Innovation includes the ongoing process of research-based continuous quality improvement of the system to ensure that the measures, the process of data collection, the integration of different standards across sectors, and the quality improvement approaches are efficient and evidence-based. Indeed, such innovation requires a dedication to ongoing research and evaluation and a commitment to a nimble enough structure to incorporate new approaches.

The final criterion is efficiency, which relates to the simplicity of the process for making decisions about QRIS policy and implementation. In an efficient governance structure, individuals with appropriate expertise make sound decisions in a timely manner. The managerial efficiency of the system can hinge on how QRIS administrators engage their partners in decisions about program standards, assessment mechanisms, data reporting, and quality improvement strategies.

As noted by Brewer and colleagues (2013), the five indicators are all desirable in theory, yet there are trade-offs between them and it is unlikely that they could be achieved simultaneously. It would be important to consider which criteria are more or less important for a QRIS to effectively have a systemic impact. A cross-state analysis of QRIS governance structures that mobilizes Brewer and Smith's framework, for instance, could help guide policymakers' efforts to strengthen QRIS' influence on the coherence of the ECE system.

CONCLUSIONS AND CONSIDERATIONS FOR FUTURE POLICYMAKING

This chapter is designed to provoke discussion about QRIS and governance. To date, early childhood practitioners, researchers, and advocates have focused on the technical dimensions of QRIS, such as setting the standards, designing the financial incentives, and developing the coaching and quality improvement strategies for participating programs. These are indeed critical decisions that have direct impacts on participating programs. We argue that the QRIS conversation should not stop there. Whether QRIS can be an effective accountability tool depends on its authority: the unity and power of its oversight structure, the legislative and regulatory underpinnings, and the use of financial incentives. There also needs to be careful thought given to the way QRIS interact with other accountability structures that are currently guiding the ECE system. QRIS may need to further coordinate efforts with school-based and Head Start accountability structures in order for the QRIS to remain viable. In sum, QRIS' potential to have a systemic and long-term impact rests on good governance.

REFERENCES

Blau, D. (2011). *The economics of early childhood education and care: Implications for the child care workforce.* Presentation at the Early Childhood Education and Care: A Workshop on February 28, 2011. Retrieved from www.iom.edu/~/media/Files/Activity%20Files/Children/EarlyChildCareEducation/Blau.pdf

Boller, K., Blair, R., Del Grosso, P., & Paulsell, D. (2010). The seeds to success modified field test: Impact evaluation findings. Retrieved from http://www.mathematica-mpr.com/~/media/publications/PDFs/earlychildhood/seeds_to_sucess_impact.pdf

Brewer, D. J., & Killeen, K. M. (2009). Organizing effective educational accountability: The case of Oklahoma. A report presented to the Oklahoma Business and Education Coalition, Tulsa, OK. Retrieved from: http://www.obecinfo.com/downloads/OKEdAccountabilityReportFinal.pdf

Brewer, D. J., Killeen, K. M., & Welsh, R. O. (2013). The role of politics and governance in educational accountability systems. *Education Finance and Policy, 8*(3), 378–393.

Brewer, D. J., & Smith, J. (2008). A framework for understanding educational governance: The case of California. *Education Finance and Policy, 3*(1), 20–40.

General Accounting Office. (2000). *Early education and care: Overlap indicates need to assess crosscutting programs.* Washington, DC: Author.

Helburn, S. W., & Bergmann, B. (2002). *America's child care problem: The way out.* New York, NY: Palgrave.

Kagan, S. L. (2006). *American early childhood education: Preventing or perpetuating inequity?* (Research Review No. 1). New York, NY: The Campaign for Educational Equity.

Kagan, S. L., & Kauerz, K. (2008). Governing American early care and education: Shifting from government to governance and from form to function. In S. Feeney, A. Galper, & C. Seefeldt (Eds.), *Continuing issues in early childhood education* (3rd ed., pp. 12–32). Columbus, OH: Pearson Merrill Prentice Hall.

Karoly, L. A., Zellman, G. L., & Perlman, M. (2013). Understanding variation in classroom quality within early childhood centers: Evidence from Colorado's quality rating and improvement system. *Early Childhood Research Quarterly, 28*(4), 645–657.

Kauerz, K., & Kagan, S. L. (2012). Governance and early childhood systems: Different forms, similar goals. In S. L. Kagan & K. Kauerz (Eds.), *Early childhood systems: Transforming early learning* (pp. 87–103). New York, NY: Teachers College Press.

Le, V., Schaack, D., & Setodji, C. M. (In press). Identifying baseline and ceiling thresholds in the Qualistar Early Learning Quality Rating and Improvement System. *Early Childhood Research Quarterly.*

Meisels, S. J., & Atkins-Burnett, S. (2006). Evaluating early childhood assessments: A differential analysis. In K. McCartney & D. Phillips (Eds.), *The Blackwell handbook of early childhood development* (pp. 533–549). Oxford, UK: Blackwell.

Mitchell, A. (2005). *Stair steps to quality: A guide for states and communities developing quality rating systems for early care and education.* Alexandria, VA: United Way of America Success by 6. Retrieved from www.earlychildhoodfinance.org/downloads/2005/MitchStairSteps_2005.pdf

Mitchell, A. (2009). *Quality rating and improvement systems as a framework for early care and education system reform*. The BUILD Initiative. Retrieved from www.earlychildhoodfinance.org/downloads/2009/QRISasSystemReform_2009.pdf

Mitchell, A. (2012). Financial incentives in quality rating and improvement systems: Approaches and effects. *QRIS National Learning Network*. Retrieved from www.qrisnetwork.org/sites/all/files/resources/gscobb/2012-05-24%2015:13/Approaches%20to%20Financial%20Incentives%20in%20QRIS.pdf

National Center on Child Care Quality Improvement. (2012). *QRIS in statutes and regulations* (No. 457). Washington, DC: Office of Child Care.

National Center on Child Care Quality Improvement. (2014). *QRIS resource guide: Section 2 Initial design process*. Washington, DC: Office of Child Care. Retrieved from https://occqrisguide.icfwebservices.com/index.cfm?do=question&sid=1&qid=159

National Early Childhood Accountability Task Force. (2007). *Taking stock: Assessing and improving early childhood learning and program quality*. Washington, DC: Pew Center on the States.

Schaack, D., Tarrant, K., Boller, K., & Tout, K. (2012). Quality rating and improvement systems: Frameworks for early care and education systems change. In S. L. Kagan & K. Kauerz (Eds.), *Early childhood systems: Looking forward, looking backward* (pp. 71–86). New York, NY: Teachers College Press.

Schultz, T. (2010). Accountability policies and transitions. In S. L. Kagan & K. Tarrant (Eds.), *Transitions in the early years: Creating a system of continuity* (pp. 267–285). Baltimore, MD: Paul H. Brookes Publishing.

Stoney, L. (2004). *Financing quality rating systems: Lessons learned*. Alexandria, VA: United Way of America Success by 6.

Tarrant, K., & Huerta, L. (In press). Substantive or symbolic stars: Quality rating and improvement systems through a new institutional lens. *Early Childhood Research Quarterly*.

Tout, K., Starr, R., Soli, M., Moodie, S., Kirby, G., & Boller, K. (2010). *Compendium of quality rating systems and evaluations*. Washington, DC: Child Trends.

Weber, M. (1958). The three types of legitimate rule (Hans Gerth, Trans.). *Berkeley Publications in Society and Institutions*, 4(1), 1–11.

Whitebook, M., Howes, C., & Phillips, D. (1990). *Who care: Child care teachers and the quality of care in America*. Washington, DC: Office of Educational Research and Improvement, U.S. Department of Education.

CHAPTER 6

Implications of Standards-Based Quality Improvement Efforts for Governance Structures

Catherine Scott-Little

Standards that define expectations for programs and the individuals participating in them have become an increasingly important element of early care and education systems. The use of standards to define how early care and education services should be delivered and the desired outcomes are a hallmark of quality improvement efforts. By setting requirements and expectations that, if met, result in high-quality early care and education programs, state-level policymakers aim to promote positive child outcomes. The increasing emphasis on standards, however, has implications for and is affected by governance structures within a state. This chapter illustrates that there has been greater pressure in the past decade for standards to be used across programs that fall under the auspices of different governance structures. Governance structures have, therefore, increasingly become salient in states' efforts to develop, implement, and monitor the use of standards. Following a brief explanation of the types of standards that are important in early care and education, this chapter discusses the relationships between governance structures and the use of standards in quality improvement efforts.

TYPES OF STANDARDS

Several types of standards play important roles within early care and education systems. This section presents a brief overview of three types of standards—program standards, early childhood educator professional competencies, and early learning and development standards. These standards have become an important part of quality improvement efforts, and, therefore, are being applied across different types of programs and governance structures. State quality enhancement efforts have been reinforced by several federal initiatives that include Good Start Grow Smart, which required states to develop voluntary early learning standards, and Race to the Top Early Learning Challenge, which required states to strengthen their early childhood infrastructure. Both of these federal initiatives encouraged states to use standards as drivers to improve program quality. In addition, Race to the Top Early Learning Challenge funding also supported states in their efforts to address governance issues to improve the quality and coordination of early education services. In the quest to use standards as drivers for quality across different types of programs, questions related to who has the authority to write and support the use of standards have emerged, and implicitly or explicitly raised questions related to governance structures.

Program Standards

For many years, the early childhood field has had different forms of standards to define requirements for program features and activities. Child-care licensing standards, often called "regulations," establish basic requirements to protect the health and safety of children and adults in child-care settings. Primarily under the purview of social service or health-related entities, these child-care program standards historically set only minimal requirements, not standards that promote quality programming (Child Care Aware of America, 2013; Office of Child Care, 2011). As publicly funded prekindergarten programs, typically housed in state departments of education, have been implemented over the past decade, program standards have become drivers to promote high-quality education experiences for children, and new entities became involved in setting standards for early education programs.

Quality Rating and Improvement Systems (QRIS) have also accelerated the emphasis on program standards as a means of promoting quality in early education settings. As of 2014, all but one state in the nation has, is piloting, or is planning a QRIS at the local or state level (QRIS National Learning Network, 2014). QRIS rely on program standards that are applied across a variety of programs to improve the quality of services for children. For instance, Minnesota's QRIS, called Parent Aware, has provisions not only for child-care programs, but also for public school prekindergarten, Head Start, and early childhood special education programs to participate.

Because QRIS include programs that fall under different auspices, governance questions regarding the authority to set and hold programs accountable for the program standards are paramount. States must consider the different types of program standards that exist in their state and decide how best to coordinate the requirements and implementation of the standards across different sectors, each of which may have its own set of standards (Office of Child Care, 2011).

Early Childhood Educator Professional Competencies

In an effort to improve program quality by bolstering the skills and knowledge of educators who work in early education programs, the majority of states have defined specific requirements for what early childhood educators should know and be able to do in order to teach young children (Winton & West, 2009). Known as Early Childhood Educator Professional Competencies (ECEPC), early childhood competencies, or core knowledge and competencies, these standards specify the knowledge and skills that persons seeking to teach in early childhood settings must demonstrate. In developing ECEPC, states have considered the national model for defining competencies for early education, the Child Development Associate (CDA), as well as their own state's requirements for early childhood programs and degrees.

This effort to improve program quality by defining standards for early educators is a relatively new development in the field. Historically, expectations for teachers have been defined through teacher licensure standards for preservice teachers enrolled in 4-year degree programs. Based on standards set by national organizations, these early childhood teacher licensure/certification requirements typically fall under the authority of state departments of education, the entities that oversee teacher licensure requirements for the K–12 education system. An increasing number of states, however, have implemented ECEPC as part of their inservice professional development and career ladder system, defining standards for inservice teachers who do not have 4-year degrees or teaching licenses (National Center for Research on Early Childhood Education [NCRECE], 2008). The quest to define expectations for what early childhood educators should know and be able to do has, therefore, spread beyond the purview of state departments of education and has extended beyond just licensed teachers to include early educators who may not have a formal degree or license to teach.

Early Learning and Development Standards

By defining what children should know and be able to do through early learning and development standards (ELDS), state agencies intend to improve the quality of early care and education programs in a number of ways. The premise is that documents that outline expectations for children's learning and development can be used to strengthen teachers' knowledge of child development, engender more intentional teaching practices, and improve the quality of professional development offered to teachers (Scott-Little, Lesko, Martella, & Milburn, 2007).

Over the past decade, the number of states with ELDS and the agencies/ entities involved in writing and implementing ELDS have increased dramatically, and the age span covered by the ELDS has likewise expanded. In 2002, only 27 states had ELDS for preschool-age children and only four states had ELDS for infants and toddlers. Furthermore, in 22 of the 27 states (81% of the states) with ELDS, the state's department of education was the lead agency responsible for writing and implementing the ELDS (Scott-Little, Kagan & Frelow, 2003). In 2002, the federal Good Start Grow Smart initiative required that the state child-care administrator develop voluntary early learning guidelines in the areas of early literacy and mathematics for preschool-age children (White House, n.d.). As a result of this federal initiative and other factors, states without ELDS had to develop them and, perhaps equally important, state child-care administrators had to engage in the ELDS writing process. The aegis for writing and implementing ELDS subsequently spread beyond the purview of state departments of education to include health and human service agencies.

DEVELOPING, IMPLEMENTING, AND MONITORING STANDARDS

Having described three types of standards, we turn now to the implications that a state's governance structure has for the development, implementation, and monitoring of standards. Key questions addressed in this section include: Who is responsible for developing standards? How does the process ensure that children and adults from diverse backgrounds are included? And where does the governance authority lie for the standards? Using examples from various states, the section illustrates different approaches based on different governance structures. Pennsylvania, in particular, is highlighted as an example of a state with a consolidated governance structure that has afforded the state the opportunity to address alignment across all three types of standards.

Development of Standards

The essence of the standards development process is agreement upon expectations for individuals or institutions—what will be required of programs, or the competencies that teachers or children will be expected to demonstrate. The process of developing standards has, in many states, been undertaken in a collaborative manner to ensure that diverse perspectives are represented in the standards, and to enhance stakeholder buy-in for the standards. There has been, however, variation in how the task of writing standards has been structured, with some states accomplishing the task through stakeholder groups convened by one lead agency and others creating a separate entity that is jointly convened by multiple agencies. This section describes different models used to develop standards, highlighting examples of how states have developed ELDS.

Models for Leadership in ELDS Writing Processes. In some states, ELDS are developed by one agency with collaboration and/or input from other agencies that also have a stake in or purview over programs that may use the standards. The lead agency typically convenes the group(s) charged with developing the standards, staffs the development process, and manages the resources used to develop the standards. The group that writes the standards often, however, includes representation from other agencies and stakeholders. For instance, the Delaware Department of Education convened an advisory work group consisting of representatives from the Delaware Health and Social Services and the Department of Services for Children, Youth and Families, as well as stakeholders from child care, higher education, and public schools, to revise the state's ELDS (Delaware Department of Education, 2010a, 2010b). In this model, the lead agency, such as the Delaware Department of Education, typically seeks support from/collaboration with other agencies, but maintains responsibility for the development process.

In states with a consolidated governance structure, responsibility for multiple types of programs falls within the purview of one agency, and so does responsibility for writing standards. In states such as Georgia, Massachusetts, and Pennsylvania, one agency oversees child-care and pre-kindergarten programs, as well as other programs related to early education, and, therefore, houses different entities that have a stake in the state's ELDS (as well as other types of standards). In these states, the task of writing standards can include staff from a variety of programs without the need for cross-agency collaboration because they all are housed within the same agency.

Representing a third model for writing standards, few states have sought to promote joint ownership of the standards writing process across multiple programs housed in different agencies without one agency taking the lead in the standards-writing process. Rather than one agency taking the lead and inviting others to participate, leadership has been provided by a group consisting of staff from multiple agencies that has been established for the purpose of writing standards. In North Carolina, for example, a task force jointly convened by the Early Childhood Advisory Council, the Division of Child Development and Early Education in the Department of Health and Human Services, and the Office of Early Learning in the Department of Public Instruction was responsible for revising the state's ELDS (North Carolina Foundations Task Force, 2013). In this case, the Task Force existed solely for the purpose of revising the ELDS, each agency included on the Task Force contributed leadership and resources, and no one agency was responsible for the process.

Implications of Standards-Writing Models. ELDS are a shared articulation of the child outcomes that a state seeks to promote—common goals for children's learning and development that are applicable across programs and governance auspices. It is, therefore, highly desirable for the task of writing ELDS to be shared across agencies, and, in fact, ELDS can bring agencies together and set the stage for shared responsibility for child outcomes. Although joint efforts to develop standards are a good strategy to improve alignment in expectations across programs and agencies, they pose governance and logistical questions and challenges if the agencies are not within the same governance structure. For instance, if the standards document is developed by multiple agencies, which agency/agencies has/have the ultimate authority and responsibility for the content? Where does the funding for the writing/revision process come from and how will it be spent efficiently? Which agency/agencies will formally adopt the standards? Who will be responsible/have the authority to decide that revisions should be made? Questions like these can be addressed in a thoughtful and collaborative manner. Nonetheless, engaging multiple agencies in writing standards can pose challenges. Furthermore, the governance structures and approaches to writing the different types of standards may vary *within* a state, providing even more reason to give careful consideration to governance issues as standards are written.

A consolidated governance structure, where one agency is responsible for multiple programs and for writing the standards that will be applied across programs, has several advantages. First, many of the governance and logistical considerations described above are irrelevant. Because one agency can bring to bear staff, resources, and stakeholders from different programs, the questions about which agency is responsible, who will take the lead, and who will fund the effort are answered—there's only one agency involved in the process.

Furthermore, if one agency has responsibility for all aspects of the early care and education system, it is easier to promote consistency/alignment across different types of standards as they are written. In Pennsylvania, for example, the Office of Child Development and Early Learning (OCDEL) consolidates responsibility for all aspects of the state's early care and education programs within one entity. As a result, the state's ELDS, core competencies for the early childhood workforce, and program quality standards are all housed within the same agency. OCDEL has, as part of its standards development and revision process, done extensive work to ensure alignment across the different types of standards, striving to ensure that the expectations for what educators should know and be able to do are aligned with what children are expected to know and be able to do, and that the standards for programs enhance educators' abilities to provide learning environments that support children's progress in the areas addressed in the ELDS (Pennsylvania OCDEL, 2013). In this case, the consolidated governance structure means not only that the ELDS standards-writing responsibility is housed within one entity, but also that OCDEL is responsible for other types of standards and can, therefore, facilitate greater alignment across expectations for children, educators, and programs as standards are written.

Supporting Implementation of Standards

To implement standards, the documents must be disseminated and providers must have opportunities to learn how to use them. Furthermore, infrastructure supports must be provided to promote the use of the standards. Questions related to governance, therefore, are also relevant for implementation of standards.

In states that implement standards through separate agencies, there is great potential for a lack of coordination and consistency in the support that providers receive. Even if standards are developed jointly or with representation from a cross-agency group, without careful coordination and strong leadership, it is common for each agency responsible for supporting providers to develop professional development separately. Some states, such as Nebraska (Nebraska Department of Education, n.d.), have developed consolidated training calendars and other mechanisms to share information about professional development being provided about the state's standards (and other topics). This is a good strategy to make educators in different programs aware of professional development that is available, but to ensure comparable professional development and support for implementation of standards across different sectors, targeted professional development must be provided to all programs. Careful planning and coordination across all agencies responsible for supporting providers is necessary to ensure that providers in all sectors of the state's service delivery system receive similar amounts of professional development and support, and that the content of the professional development is consistent from program to program.

Within a consolidated governance model, where one agency oversees all early childhood programs, training and support to promote the use of the standards can be designed and implemented consistently across different sectors. Pennsylvania, for instance, has established a system that provides professional development to all early childhood programs, regardless of funding source or program type. Child care, Head Start, public school, and Early Intervention staff receive professional development and are included in the state's career ladder system, known as Pennsylvania Keys to Professional Development (Pennsylvania Early Learning Keys to Quality, n.d.). Furthermore, Pennsylvania has developed Core Competencies for professional development providers to ensure that the training, technical assistance, and coaching provided in the state are aligned with the state's standards, and to promote consistency across the professional development providers that support programs (Pennsylvania OCDEL, 2013). Having a consolidated governance structure means that support for implementing program standards, ECEPC standards, and ELDS all rest within the same entity, facilitating a coordinated and aligned approach to supporting providers as they implement the standards.

Monitoring and Accountability for Standards

For standards to achieve their potential as drivers to improve program quality and to support positive child outcomes, there must be a system for monitoring the degree to which the standards are met. For program standards, this means that states must establish a system to document how programs meet structural requirements, such as group sizes and ratios, and process requirements, such as positive adult-child interactions. For ECEPC standards, a system is needed to evaluate individual teachers to ensure that they have received specified professional development and that they possess the knowledge and skills articulated in the standards. Finally, monitoring the use of ELDS can include both requirements for documentation that the ELDS are used in curriculum planning, and child outcome data to determine if children are making progress on the standards and indicators articulated in the ELDS document.

Oversight for the use of each of these types of standards can be the focus of different agencies and entities, but a coordinated accountability system is the most cohesive and efficient way to hold programs accountable for meeting the standards. Without some mechanism for coordinating how programs are held accountable for meeting standards, there can be unevenness in the type of data/documentation used to determine whether programs meet the standards and in the degree to which programs are held accountable. Furthermore, multiple agencies must invest time and resources in developing separate monitoring and data collection systems.

States' QRIS could potentially be a mechanism to monitor the extent to which programs meet all three types of standards. Pennsylvania's Keystone STARS QRIS is an example of a coordinated approach (Pennsylvania OCDEL, 2013). The OCDEL has the responsibility for monitoring programs to determine the extent to which they meet the program standards. OCDEL also is responsible for the Pennsylvania Early Learning Keys to Quality Career Lattice, which sets minimum requirements for different types of positions and for the system used to document the extent to which educators demonstrate proficiency on the Core Knowledge ECPC established in the state. In addition, programs are required to conduct ongoing child assessments using tools that are aligned with the state's ELDS, and state-funded programs, including those that are participating in the upper levels of the state's QRIS, must submit child outcomes results to a centralized data system. Pennsylvania has a long-term goal of coordinating program monitoring to include data on the extent to which programs meet the programs standards, staff meet the Core Knowledge requirements, and children are making progress on the state's ELDS (Pennsylvania OCDEL, 2013).

Using the QRIS as the mechanism for accountability, however, means that the QRIS must include requirements related to all three types of standards and that programs operated under different auspices must participate in the QRIS. Without these conditions, oversight for the implementation of standards may address only a limited scope of the standards that are required, or may hold just a limited number or certain types of programs accountable. Governance issues, therefore, have important implications for how compliance with standards is monitored.

CONSIDERATIONS AND IMPLICATIONS

Program improvement efforts, program standards, Early Childhood Educator Professional Competencies (ECEPC), and the use of early learning and development standards (ELDS) should go hand in hand, and, when they are consistent or aligned with one another, the efforts to improve programs are strengthened and children and families are better served. As we have seen in this chapter, each of these types of standards is being applied across different types of programs, and there is, therefore, increasing momentum for multiple agencies to be involved in all aspects of setting and implementing standards. Our early childhood silos, with child care answering to one set of standards and other programs answering to different standards, are being dismantled and reconfigured as program standards, ECEPCs, and ELDS are applied across programs. Cross-program and cross-governance efforts to improve the quality of care through standards that are applied across service sectors hold great potential for aligning expectations, evening out the support that is available across different programs, and equalizing the extent to which programs are held accountable for meeting standards. There are, however, numerous issues that need to be addressed to develop a standards-based, coordinated early childhood system.

One issue to address is the governance structure within the state. Consideration must be given to which agency has the authority over the standards and to what extent that agency has the authority to enforce them across different types of programs. Given that states are relying heavily on their QRIS to document and evaluate program quality, it would seem that the agency responsible for the QRIS might be a natural choice for standards-setting and monitoring. In many states, however, the QRIS is still in the early stages of development and the number of programs, as well as the types of programs, participating may be limited. Furthermore, other systems, such as the state's prekindergarten and/or early intervention programs, may already be entrenched in their own standards, professional development supports, and monitoring systems. Therefore, the effort to consolidate standards and the authority to hold programs accountable for meeting or using standards would require either solid agreements between different agencies or a major change in the governance structure of the state's early childhood services.

Variation in the resources available to different programs is a second issue that must be addressed before/as a state pursues a standards-based system of quality improvement across different programs. Historically, child-care programs have had fewer resources, less-qualified staff, and more demands to provide services to a wider age range of children for more hours than other programs that may provide part-day and/or part-year programs to a specific target population, such as 4-year-olds or children with disabilities (Stoney & Greenberg, 1996). Expecting child-care programs, or other programs with fewer resources and greater demands for services, to meet the same standards as programs that have higher levels of funding or that provide services on a more limited basis may be unfair. Inequities in resources available to different types of programs must be taken into account as standards are set and supports provided to programs to help them meet standards. Lower-resourced programs may deserve accommodations to meet the standards and greater support through training and technical assistance systems.

Finally, the extent to which the standards reflect the diversity of the programs and the children and families served in different programs is a consideration. Many states have sought stakeholder input as they have developed standards, and this effort to reflect stakeholder values is laudable. Yet, in the effort to develop standards that will be applied across multiple programs, there is the possibility that the perspectives of the specific populations served in specific programs may have been diluted or lost as the number of programs and stakeholder perspectives incorporated into the development process grows. Therefore, as efforts to develop and apply standards across programs emerge, greater care must be taken to ensure that the perspectives of all stakeholders are represented in the development process to certify that the standards are applicable for the diverse populations served across different programs.

Although one might argue that program-specific standards can be tailored to the needs of service providers within the specific program, continuing to implement program-specific standards may perpetuate inequalities between programs and, in turn, inequalities in the services that children and families receive. In the age of standards-based early childhood services, we must address the governance questions that emerge as standards are applied across multiple programs to ensure access to the highest quality of services for children, regardless of the program in which they are enrolled.

REFERENCES

Child Care Aware of America. (2013). *We can do better: Child Care Aware of America's ranking of state child care center regulations and oversight.* Arlington, VA: Author. Retrieved from www.naccrra.org/sites/default/files/default_site_pages/2013/wcdb_2013_final_april_11_0.pdf

Delaware Department of Education. (2010a). *Delaware early learning foundations: Infant/toddler.* Dover, DE: Author. Retrieved from www.doe.k12.de.us/infosuites/students_family/earlychildhood/elg.shtml

Delaware Department of Education. (2010b). *Delaware early learning foundations: Preschool.* Dover, DE: Author. Retrieved from www.doe.k12.de.us/infosuites/students_family/earlychildhood/elg.shtml

National Center for Research on Early Childhood Education (NCRECE). (2008). *Ensuring effective teaching in early childhood education through linked professional development systems, quality rating systems and state competencies: The role of research in an evidence-driven system.* Charlottesville, VA: Author.

Nebraska Department of Education. (n.d.). *Early childhood training center.* Retrieved from www.education.ne.gov/oec/ectc.html

North Carolina Foundations Task Force. (2013). *North Carolina foundations for early learning and development.* Raleigh, NC: Author. Retrieved from http://ncchildcare.nc.gov/pdf_forms/NC_foundations.pdf

Office of Child Care. (2011). *A foundation for quality improvement systems: State licensing, preschool, and QRIS program quality standards.* Washington, DC: Author. Retrieved from www.qrisnetwork.org/sites/all/files/resources/gscobb/2012-03-19%2012%3A52/Report.pdf

Parent Aware. (n.d.). *Public school prekindergarten and head start applications.* Retrieved from http://parentawareratings.org/public-school-pre-kindergarten-and-head-start-applicants

Pennsylvania Early Learning Keys to Quality. (n.d.). *Career development.* Retrieved from www.pakeys.org/pages/get.aspx?page=Career

Pennsylvania Office of Child Development and Early Learning (OCDEL). (2013). *Child care and development fund (CCDF) plan for Pennsylvania 2014–2015.* Harrisburg, PA: Author. Retrieved from www.dpw.state.pa.us/dpworganization/officeofchilddevelopmentandearlylearning/

QRIS National Learning Network. (2014, August). *Current status of QRIS in states.* Retrieved from http://qrisnetwork.org/~qris/qris-state-contacts-map

Scott-Little, C., Kagan, S. L., & Frelow, V. S. (2003, Fall). Creating the conditions for success with early learning standards: Results from a national study of state-level standards for children's learning prior to kindergarten. *Early Childhood Research and Practice.* 5(2). Retrieved from http://ecrp.uiuc.edu/v5n2/little.html

Scott-Little, C., Lesko, J., Martella, J., & Milburn, P. (2007). Early learning standards: Results from a national survey to document trends in state-level policies and practices. *Early Childhood Research and Practice, 9*(1). Retrieved from http://ecrp.uiuc.edu/v9n1/little.html

Stoney, L., & Greenberg, M. H. (1996). The financing of child care: Current and emerging trends. *The Future of Children, 6* (2), 83–102.

White House. (n.d.). *Good start, grow smart: The Bush administration's early childhood initiative.* Retrieved from http://georgewbush-whitehouse.archives.gov/infocus/earlychildhood/earlychildhood.html

Winton, P., & West, T. (2009). *Competencies for early childhood educators in the context of inclusion: Issues and guidance for states.* Chapel Hill, NC: Frank Porter Graham Institute.

CHAPTER 7

Early Childhood Governance and Accountability

Thomas Schultz

Issues of governance and accountability are tightly intertwined, both conceptually and in the real world of public policy for young children (defined in this chapter as birth through 3rd grade). Our governance system (defined as decisionmaking and leadership efforts of federal and state legislators and executive branch officials) is replete with efforts to provide accountability to citizens on the performance of all forms of publicly funded programs. Accordingly, policy leaders concerned with improving early childhood–3rd grade learning opportunities and outcomes devote considerable time and energy to accountability issues. For example, as they develop early childhood program or education reform legislation, federal and state legislators debate and determine multiple accountability-related provisions, such definitions of program outcomes, eligible participants, service strategies, allowable uses of funding, and requirements in the areas of standards, assessments, reporting systems, and program evaluation. Similarly, implementing accountability mandates is a central priority for state and federal early childhood and public education agency leaders, including their work in promulgating and monitoring compliance with regulations, managing assessment and program monitoring systems, and administering performance-based incentives and technical assistance efforts.

Early childhood accountability systems perform important functions and influence birth–3rd grade educators in a variety of ways. They provide feedback on the overall performance of our early education and public education systems and on the extent to which they improve over time. They support the idea of linking consequences to program performance. They function as a continuous improvement system, motivated and guided by standards-based assessment data. They define priorities for teachers and administrators, and shape the normative climate of their work. They also impose substantial costs in dollars and staff time on local programs and schools to administer assessments, undergo on-site reviews, complete reports, and implement program improvement efforts.

In sum, accountability is a major function of our governance system, accountability policies derive from decisionmaking and leadership efforts by government leaders, and accountability mandates have a substantial influence on local birth–3rd grade programs and practitioners.

This chapter argues that federal and state policymakers have created a framework of accountability policies with key structural defects and shortcomings. It then discusses the extent to which proposed reforms in early childhood governance are likely to foster progress toward a more coherent, effective, and efficient accountability system for birth–3rd grade care and education, concluding that current proposals for reforming early childhood governance are likely to generate only incremental solutions to our fundamental accountability challenges.

EARLY CHILDHOOD ACCOUNTABILITY: WHERE WE STAND

Although birth–3rd grade accountability initiatives adhere to a common conceptual framework, as summarized in Figure 7.1, they comprise an exceedingly complex policy landscape, based on policy decisions to fund birth–3rd grade care and education services through multiple categorical programs, managed by a variety of state and federal agencies. In fact, as shown in Table 7.1, this governance approach has created at least five parallel accountability systems, managed by different departments, agencies, and program offices. This overview could be expanded to incorporate standards, assessments, and program improvement efforts linked to early childhood programs funded through the Elementary and Secondary Education Act (ESEA) Title I, a new federal Evidence-Based Home Visitation Program, and varied state-funded parent education, Grade Level Reading, and family literacy programs.

Early childhood accountability policy is further complicated by the differing structural arrangements for the oversight of local early childhood agencies and kindergarten–3rd grade schooling. That is, child-care, early childhood special education, and kindergarten–3rd grade programs are funded and managed via federal-to-state-to-local arrangements, Head Start through a federal-to-local approach (with no state involvement), and state pre-K programs in state-to-local relationships (with no federal involvement). This means that local programs contend with multiple, uncoordinated accountability initiatives and reforms, one right after the other.

Figure 7.1. Early Childhood Accountability Conceptual Framework

Define Standards

for desired developmental and learning outcomes for children and for program quality and teaching practices

Collect and Report Assessment Data

on children's learning and development and program/teaching quality

Manage Program Improvement Efforts

including systems of incentives, sanctions, or technical assistance to improve program quality and outcomes for children

Multiple uncoordinated early childhood accountability policies lead to two daunting challenges: first, the costs and complications of managing multiple systems of standards, assessments, data, and technical assistance; and second, the use of divergent accountability paradigms in programs for children, birth through age 5 versus for kindergarten–3rd grade students (National Early Childhood Accountability Task Force, 2007; Schultz, 2014).

Managing Multiple Accountability Mandates

The challenge of implementing multiple accountability mandates occurs because many local early childhood agencies and school districts receive funding from several federal or state programs to support children from birth through 3rd grade (Wallen & Hubbard, 2013). Local administrators then must demonstrate compliance with varied sets of child outcome and program quality standards, administer several assessments, undergo multiple program monitoring reviews, and report to varied program offices. Simply understanding the content of a number of voluminous and dense accountability policy documents is a daunting challenge; for example, Head Start has more than 2,400 program quality standards (U.S. Department of Health and Human Services, 2009), and California's Preschool Learning Foundations consists of three separate volumes, totaling more than 580 pages (California Department of Education, 2008, 2010, 2012).

Teachers also face challenges in striving to implement multiple sets of standards and assessments. Many teachers of preschool children work with not only their state early learning guidelines, but also with the Office of

Table 7.1. Current Early Childhood Accountability Policies

	Child Care	Head Start/ Early Head Start	Early Childhood Special Education	State Pre-K	Kindergarten to Grade 3
Oversight & Management	HHS—Office of Child Care	HHS—Office of Head Start	ED—Office of Special Ed. Services	State Agencies	ED
Child Development/ Learning Standards	State Early Learning Guidelines	Federal Child Outcomes Framework	Federal standards call for assessing children in five developmental domains	State Early Learning Guidelines	Common Core State Standards (Language Arts & Mathematics) + Additional State Standards
Program Quality Standards	State Licensing Standards (Mandatory) QRIS Quality Standards (Voluntary)	Federal Program Performance Standards	Federal IDEA regulations	State Program Standards	School Accreditation Standards
Child Assessments	No requirements	Local agencies define school readiness goals and analyze assessment data at three points in the program year	Programs assess children in five domains, in areas of delay or suspected disabilities and on three functional outcomes	Varied state policies and tools	Kindergarten Entry Assessments Assessments for reading on grade level Assessments to inform teacher evaluations
Program Quality Assessments	State Quality Rating and Improvement Systems State licensing reviews	Federal monitoring of local program compliance with Performance Standards CLASS tool measures classroom/teaching quality	Federal reviews of states State reviews of local programs	State monitoring of local programs	School accreditation reviews Personnel evaluations include measures of teaching practices/quality
Reporting/Use of Assessment Data	QRIS Ratings linked to funding incentives and technical assistance Violations of licensing standards can lead to closing of facilities	Programs receive technical assistance to remedy program quality problems. Low-performing programs may be defunded or required to recompete for funding.	States report on State Performance Plans on program quality and child outcomes goals. States report on children's progress in three functional goals, in relation to same-aged peers.	Varied approaches to technical assistance or enforcement of quality standards	Persistently low-performing schools are targeted for technical assistance or restructuring. Value-added student assessment data outcomes are used in teacher evaluations and personnel decisions.

Notes: CLASS = Classroom Assessment Scoring System; HHS = Health and Human Services.

Head Start's Child Development and Early Learning Framework and/or the Office of Special Education's functional child outcomes document (U.S. Department of Health and Human Services, 2010a, 2010b). Similarly, many kindergarten teachers are administering kindergarten entry assessments as well as assessments tied to Grade Level Reading initiatives, teacher evaluation systems, and implementation of the Common Core State Standards. These ambitious expectations for teachers are particularly problematic because inherent in accountability policy is the hope that teachers will use assessment data not only for accountability reporting but also to guide their work with children. It is hard, however, for teachers to plan standards-based and assessment-informed curricula if they work in settings governed by multiple accountability systems.

Divergent Accountability Paradigms for Different Age Groups

A second key problem with current early childhood accountability policies is that of divergent accountability paradigms for programs for children birth to age 5 versus kindergarten–3rd grade education (Schultz, 2008). These differences begin with the disjuncture between focusing on program quality metrics in birth–age 5 program accountability, and focusing on outcomes-based accountability in kindergarten–3rd grade education. Program quality–based accountability systems have been in place in child care, Head Start, state prekindergarten, and early childhood special education programs for decades, whereas there are only a few instances of use of child assessment data in birth–age 5 accountability initiatives, and the use of assessment data on young children in accountability systems is a highly contentious issue (Meisels, 2006; National Early Childhood Accountability Task Force, 2007; Snow & Van Hemel, 2008). By contrast, the dominant accountability paradigm in public education relies on student assessment data (although accountability-mandated assessments are limited to students in grades 3 and beyond) (Regenstein & Romero-Jurado, 2014). The state of Florida utilizes the results of a kindergarten entry assessment in its accountability system for the state pre-K program, and the state of Louisiana is currently developing an accountability initiative for its child-care and pre-K programs that entails use of a standardized assessment of classroom quality and a child assessment tool (Florida Department of Education, 2013). However, these initiatives are the only current instances of using child assessment data in high-stakes accountability systems for programs for children from birth through age 5.

Other differences in accountability policies between the birth–age 5 and kindergarten–3rd grade sectors include differing approaches to the use of incentives (public education accountability relies primarily on sanctions for persistently low-performing schools versus early childhood Quality Rating and Improvement Systems [QRIS] that provide higher rates of funding to reward higher-performing agencies) and standards (kindergarten–3rd grade standards focus on curriculum content areas versus birth–age 5 standards, which are organized around domains of child development), and public education's new emphasis on outcomes-based teacher and administrator evaluation systems, which is not a current focus in accountability policy in programs for younger children. These differing accountability approaches, metrics, and vocabulary make it difficult for colleagues from birth–age 5 programs to work with kindergarten–3rd grade practitioners on shared priorities, such as ensuring that children are optimally prepared for kindergarten and that they are on track in relation to standards for early learning and child development across the birth–3rd grade years (Kauerz & Coffman, 2013; Zellman & Karoly, 2012).

REFORMING BIRTH–3RD GRADE ACCOUNTABILITY POLICIES

In sum, rather than establishing a unified and coherent early childhood accountability system, state and federal government policy leaders have created a conglomeration of standards, assessments, and program improvement systems and divergent accountability approaches to documenting and improving the performance of programs for children prior to kindergarten versus kindergarten–3rd grade students. This mix of policies may be well suited to documenting compliance with specific state and federal program mandates, but it is costly and complex for local early childhood administrators and teachers to navigate. Furthermore, it fails to provide early childhood professionals with a shared conception of desired outcomes for children or a common vision of a high-quality, engaging, and powerful continuum of teaching and learning opportunities across the birth–3rd grade years.

The complexity and contradictions of early childhood accountability policy have given rise to a variety of reform proposals. These initiatives share a systemic perspective, highlighting the common purpose of early childhood–3rd grade education programs and the common cause of improving the quality, effectiveness, and outcomes of all early childhood–3rd grade settings, regardless of their funding source. Three key strategies are being pursued to improve the coherence, effectiveness, and efficiency of early childhood accountability policies:

- Aligning and mapping child and program quality accountability standards

- Linking and simplifying accountability mechanisms
- Building networks among birth–3rd grade teachers and leaders

Aligning and Mapping

Aligning child and program quality standards horizontally (across programs serving children of the same age) and vertically (across the birth–3rd grade continuum) addresses standards as the foundation of accountability-related assessments and program improvement efforts. Mapping varied standards frameworks highlights patterns of similarities, inconsistencies, gaps, and redundancies across the standards and draws attention to their collective expectations for children, programs, and teachers. Standards alignment efforts include efforts by states to develop a composite set of standards for preschool-age children that incorporate Head Start and Office of Special Education Programs outcomes as well as state early learning guidelines. In addition, states are working to improve the vertical alignment of standards for infants, toddlers, preschoolers, and kindergarten–3rd grade students (Cooper & Costa, 2012; Kagan & Scott-Little, 2004; Scott-Little, Kagan, Frelow, & Reid, 2009). The goals of vertical alignment are several:

- To create a smooth progression of standards, so that standards for younger children include precursor skills that prepare them for expectations in subsequent years
- To eliminate repetition or overlap in standards from a particular year or developmental period to the next
- To promote congruence in content of standards, so that standards for kindergarten–3rd grade students continue the emphasis in birth–age 5 standards on children's social and emotional development, physical development, and approaches to learning

States are also engaged in mapping program quality standards, to identify the extent to which different state and federal programs share similar standards, provide for unique standards in specific areas, or have set standards at varying levels of quality or rigor.

Linking and Simplifying

A second focus of early childhood accountability reform efforts is linking and simplifying accountability mechanisms in areas such as child and program quality assessments, data systems, and technical assistance efforts. For example, many states are creating Quality Rating and Improvement

Systems to improve programs for children birth to age 5 by creating multi-tiered systems of program quality standards (Lahti, Sabol, Starr, Langill, & Tout, 2013; Mead, 2013; Mitchell, 2009; Tout et al., 2010; Tout, Zaslow, Halle, & Forry, 2009). Although they began as a strategy to improve child-care services, they also strive to be inclusive of program quality standards and accountability efforts in other publicly funded programs for young children. Thus, QRIS initiatives provide opportunity to create consolidated frameworks of program quality standards that cross-reference requirements from different state and federal funding streams. They could also provide reciprocity for program quality assessments carried out by different state and federal agencies. Thus, if a local agency demonstrates compliance with Head Start or state pre-K program quality standards, it could receive credit for this level of performance within the QRIS system. Such programs would only be required to undergo assessment of QRIS quality standards that were covered in their prior monitoring review.

States are also making efforts to link early childhood data systems across federal and state programs for birth–age 5 children, as well as vertically with longitudinal education data systems for kindergarten–3rd grade students and beyond (Early Childhood Data Collaborative, 2010). Linking data systems could reduce the need for program managers, teachers, or families to enter the same information multiple times in reporting systems for different state or federal programs. Linking data on children, early childhood programs, and teachers also enables policy leaders to view "undupli-cated counts" of children who are enrolled in various early learning programs, a cumulative picture of the early childhood workforce, and data on program quality from different accountability systems. Finally, coordinated birth–3rd grade data systems enable kindergarten–3rd grade teachers to see a picture of children's participation in early childhood programs (as well as data from assessments carried out by those programs), and for early childhood agencies to obtain information from elementary schools on how the children they have served are progressing in kindergarten–3rd grade classrooms and beyond. Data linkage efforts could also lead, over time, to efforts to simplify or consolidate reporting requirements from different early childhood funding streams (Hernandez, 2012).

Building Networks

A third strategy to overcome the balkanized nature of early childhood accountability policies is building professional networks to engage educators across categorical program types and across the birth–3rd grade years in collaborative, standards-based program improvement efforts. For instance,

state and federal agency staff members could engage in joint program monitoring reviews in instances where they are providing funding to the same
school districts or local early childhood agencies. Shared monitoring efforts would help reviewers become familiar with their varied approaches
to documenting performance on program quality standards. Over time,
joint monitoring teams could identify opportunities to streamline review
procedures or support efforts to pool technical assistance by different state
and federal program offices. Local agencies could benefit because it would
take less time to participate in a single monitoring process versus multiple
reviews at different points in time. They also would benefit from receiving
a single, comprehensive summary of their strengths and weaknesses, and a
single statement of priorities for program improvement.

Another example of networking efforts to overcome the adverse effects
of siloed accountability policies is pre-K–3rd grade initiatives involving
"vertical teams" of preschool, kindergarten, 1st- through 3rd-grade teachers, and program administrators. These networks build a shared awareness
of the continuum of birth–3rd grade standards and assessments of children,
programs, and teachers; engage teams in studying longitudinal assessment
data on children and the quality of teaching practices; and promote joint
planning of curricula, family engagement, and professional development efforts (Kauerz & Coffman, 2013; Mead, 2009; Tout, Halle, Daily, Albertson-
Junkans, & Moodie, 2013).

Table 7.2 summarizes the three reform strategies and how they respond
to the challenges of multiple accountability systems and divergent paradigms.

Taken together, these reforms can provide a variety of benefits to teachers and local birth–3rd grade program administrators, including:

- Clearer signals on desired outcomes and best practices in their
  daily work with young children and families, rather than separate
  versions of our goals for each type of federal and state program

Table 7.2. Reforming Early Childhood Accountability Policies and Systems

Reform Strategies	Remedies for Fragmented Accountability Policies	Remedies for Bifurcated Accountability Policies
Align child and program quality standards	Horizontal alignment of standards	Vertical alignment of standards
Link and simplify accountability mechanisms	QRIS	
	Link data across birth–age 5 programs	Link birth–3rd grade data systems
Build birth–3rd grade professional networks	Joint program monitoring	P–3rd grade teams of teachers and program managers

- Reducing costs and eliminating duplication of effort for local programs
- Accelerating progress toward a shared conception of accountability among teachers and administrators, as well as a culture of shared responsibility among early childhood–3rd grade teachers to ensure children's progress toward standards

EARLY CHILDHOOD GOVERNANCE
AND ACCOUNTABILITY REFORM

To what extent can reforming early childhood governance contribute to re- solving the central challenges of fragmented and bifurcated early childhood accountability policies? As treated in more depth in other chapters, early childhood governance reform efforts have focused on improving state-level oversight, management, and leadership of the varied programs and fund- ing streams serving children birth through age 5. These reforms address problems arising from states dispersing responsibility for managing birth– age 5 programs among a variety of agencies—typically housing child-care programs in human service or workforce agencies, state pre-K and special education in departments of education, and special education for infants and toddlers and home visitation programs in health departments. Thus, the rationale for governance reforms corresponds closely to our analysis of the problem of fragmented accountability efforts. That is, proposals for reforming state governance of programs for children birth to age 5 are in- tended to promote greater coherence, alignment, and coordination of poli- cies across categorical programs; to reduce duplication of effort and im- prove efficiency in program management; and to enhance accountability for early childhood program performance (Florida Office of Program Policy Analysis & Government Accountability, 2008; Kagan & Kauerz, 2009, 2012; Regenstein & Lipper, 2013).

As summarized in Chapter 3, states have pursued three approaches to early childhood governance reform:

- *Coordination:* Developing new mechanisms to encourage collaboration among state agencies responsible for managing birth– age 5 early childhood programs
- *Consolidation:* Designating a single current state agency to manage all early childhood programs
- *Creation:* Creating a new state agency to manage all early childhood programs

Each of these options is likely to accelerate progress in addressing the challenge of multiple, uncoordinated accountability policies in programs for children birth to age 5. For several reasons, co-locating birth–age 5 programs in a current or new state agency or strengthening mechanisms for interagency collaboration would make it more likely to implement reforms such as horizontal alignment of child outcomes and program quality standards, inclusive QRIS, linking data across birth–age 5 programs, and joint program monitoring efforts.

First, when states adopt any of these governance reforms, it means they are placing a priority on enhancing the coordination of policy and management across birth–age 5 programs, including issues of accountability. Second, each of these governance reforms creates new leadership positions with responsibility for all early childhood programs, or for cross-agency collaboration in the case of the coordination option. These changes would clarify and centralize responsibility for documenting and improving the performance of all early care and education programs. Arguably, senior managers in these positions would be naturally inclined to take note of the costs and complications of managing multiple accountability systems and be receptive to reforms such as aligning child and program quality standards, and linking or developing a common data or technical assistance system. Third, these options—in particular, the consolidation and creation approaches—create new opportunities for mid-level program managers and staff members to work together in new ways across funding streams. Co-location of staff members increases opportunities for collaboration on functions such as program monitoring, professional development, and technical assistance. In addition, having staff members work in the same agency would contribute to building a common culture for program accountability and program improvement efforts, rather than staff being oriented primarily to the accountability ethos of particular categorical programs. Fourth, these structural options could make it easier for local early childhood providers, including school districts, to engage with a single point of contact on issues of early childhood accountability policy.

Finally, although the primary purpose of early childhood governance reforms is to improve state leadership and oversight of birth–age 5 programs, it is also important to consider how these reforms would address the problem of bifurcated accountability policies between the birth–age 5 and kindergarten–3rd grade sectors. For example, it would be easier and less complex to align birth–age 5, kindergarten–3rd grade, and accountability policies and systems if leadership for birth–age 5 programs were centralized or more strongly coordinated. However, governance reforms to create new state agencies for birth–age 5 services could also detract from cross-pollination and collaboration on accountability policy across the birth–age 5 and kindergarten–3rd grade sectors. That is, moving birth–age 5 programs from state departments of education (SDEs) to new freestanding state early childhood agencies would detract from opportunities for collaboration on accountability efforts between SDE staff members responsible for birth–age 5 programs and colleagues responsible for kindergarten–3rd grade teaching and learning policy. On the other hand, if states consolidated responsibility for all birth–age 5 programs within the state department of education, progress on the challenge of divergent birth–age 5 and kindergarten–3rd grade accountability paradigms could be accelerated.

In this same vein, it is appropriate to note that any proposed structure for state management of programs represents a trade-off in terms of opportunities to promote collaboration and a sense of shared purpose among state managers, staff members, and their local program counterparts. For example, locating early care and education programs in a state human service, family support, or workforce development agency could promote collaborative efforts around the goal of two-generational program strategies to enhance early childhood development in context with family support, family literacy, and economic development efforts. Similarly, housing all programs for infants, toddlers, preschoolers, and children and youth with disabilities within a single agency could enhance opportunities for supporting a more seamless and well-coordinated continuum of services for those children.

THE LIMITS OF INCREMENTAL REFORM

Our current early childhood system is the result of decades of decisions by states and the federal government to support young children, birth to age 5, through an array of categorical programs followed by a separately funded and governed universal public education system for kindergarten–3rd grade children. Thus far, this chapter has described how this governance approach has led to fragmented and bifurcated birth–3rd grade accountability efforts, and how state-level early childhood governance reform could create a more congenial environment for improving early childhood accountability through reforms, including mapping and aligning child and program quality standards, linking and simplifying accountability mechanisms, and building networks among state and local birth–3rd grade program managers and staff members.

Before concluding, however, it is important to observe that this reform agenda is only an incremental response to the root causes of complexity and incoherence in early childhood accountability policy. That is, even if fully implemented, these accountability and governance reform proposals would not alter the multiple state and federal funding streams for early education, the structural divide between birth–age 5 and kindergarten–3rd grade programs, or the problem of dispersed authority for early childhood accountability policy between federal and state governments.

For example, states can map and align child and program quality standards, but they do not have the authority to waive standards that are attached to federal categorical programs. QRIS, data system linkages, and joint monitoring efforts do not eliminate program-specific data systems or requirements to document compliance with program-specific legislative mandates and regulations. And vertical alignment of standards, linking early childhood and longitudinal education data systems and pre-K–3rd grade initiatives do not reconcile the fundamental conflict between early childhood's reliance on program quality–based accountability and public education's devotion to outcomes-based accountability. Although current accountability reform ideas may be creative work-arounds to address the shortcomings of our early governance system, they may chart a pathway that will leave us only marginally better off—adding an overlay of coordinating mechanisms on top of fundamentally fragmented programs and policies.

Moreover, these core structural features of early childhood governance and accountability policy are being reinforced by recent federal initiatives and investments. The Race to the Top–Early Learning Challenge Fund (RTT–ELC) is certainly the most notable of these efforts because it is providing roughly $1 billion to 20 states for cross-program systems-building and infrastructure efforts, including projects to implement the accountability reform strategies described in this chapter, such as creating inclusive QRIS systems, aligning early learning and kindergarten–3rd grade standards, building comprehensive child and program assessment systems, and linking early childhood and public education data systems (U.S. Department of Education, 2013). Yet paradoxically, this historic investment is largely aimed at funding states to overcome policy challenges that are generated largely by federal program structures and management practices that remain largely unchanged. That is, there is not a concomitant federal effort to develop coordinated standards for children or program quality, nor common systems in the areas of program monitoring, data, professional development, or technical assistance across Head Start, child care, early childhood special education, and other federal programs.

The further irony is that, while the Early Learning Challenge initiative is building more unified state early learning systems across categorical programs, the federal government is simultaneously initiating additional new categorical programs, including evidence-based home visitation initiative, Promise Neighborhoods, Early Head Start–Child Care Partnerships, and Preschool Development and Expansion Grants programs, each with new legislative mandates and regulations around issues of program accountability.

Similarly, the federal government is continuing to support divergent approaches to accountability policy for birth–age 5 and kindergarten–3rd grade education. Indeed, the Obama administration has funded two separate initiatives to reform public education and early childhood accountability practices. The Race to the Top school reform initiative includes initiatives that influence the work of kindergarten–3rd grade educators, and the Race to the Top–Early Learning Challenge strategy addresses programs for children birth–age 5, although it does also support some state efforts to link policies across the birth–3rd grade continuum.

If on target, this analysis poses a central challenge for the early childhood community and public policy leaders: whether to continue the current system of multiple categorical programs or to advocate for a more systemic structure for early childhood governance, finance, and management. This choice raises fundamental questions, such as:

- To what extent do the purposes and target populations of current categorical early childhood programs require different outcome standards for children or different standards for program quality?
- To what extent is a shared strategy for accountability across the birth–3rd grade years feasible and desirable? Is there room for common ground between birth–age 5 program quality–oriented accountability and kindergarten–3rd grade outcomes-based accountability?
- What is the appropriate division of responsibility among federal, state, and local governments in decisionmaking on issues of early childhood accountability?

CONCLUSIONS

In conclusion, current ideas for reforming early childhood governance and accountability derive from a common diagnosis of the complications and inadequacies of our present system of funding and managing education programs for young children. Unless early childhood leaders propose more fundamental reforms, however, progress toward a unified, efficient, and powerful approach to early childhood accountability will be limited. It is time for a national debate on whether our current structure of multiple categorical programs and divergent approaches to governing birth–age 5 and kindergarten–3rd grade education is best for the future. Fortunately, this debate is what our governance system is designed to address and resolve—one way or another.

NOTE

Albert Wat provided valuable help in conceptualizing and developing this chapter and Lisa Guernsey, Anne Mitchell, and Elliott Regenstein provided helpful comments on an earlier draft.

REFERENCES

California Department of Education. (2008). *Preschool learning foundations: Volume 1*. Sacramento, CA: Author.

California Department of Education. (2010). *Preschool learning foundations: Volume 2*. Sacramento, CA: Author.

California Department of Education. (2012). *Preschool learning foundations: Volume 3*. Sacramento, CA: Author.

Cooper, D., & Costa, K. (2012). *Increasing the effectiveness and efficiency of existing public investments in early childhood education*. Washington, DC: Center for American Progress.

Early Childhood Data Collaborative. (2010). *Building and using coordinated state early care and education data systems: A framework for state policymakers*. Washington, DC: Author. Retrieved from www.dataqualitycampaign.org. resources/1007

Florida Department of Education. (2013). *Kindergarten assessment: History and legislative authority*. Tallahassee, FL: Office of Early Learning. Retrieved from www.floridaearlylearning.com/sites/www/Uploads/HistoryOfKindergarten AssessmentInFlorida.pdf

Florida Office of Program Policy Analysis & Government Accountability. (2008). *The governance structure of Florida's early education programs presents some administrative challenges*. Tallahassee, FL: Author.

Hernandez, D. J. (2012). *PreK–3rd: New steps for state longitudinal data systems*. New York, NY: Foundation for Child Development.

Kagan, S. L., & Kauerz, K. (2009). Governing American early care and education: Shifting from government to governance and from form to function. In S. Feeney, A. Galper, & C. Seefeldt (Eds.), *Continuing issues in early childhood education* (3rd ed., pp. 12–32). Upper Saddle River, NJ: Pearson.

Kagan, S. L., & Kauerz, K. (Eds.) (2012). *Early childhood systems: Transforming early learning*. New York, NY: Teachers College Press.

Kagan, S. L., & Scott-Little, C. (2004). Early learning standards: Changing the parlance and practice of early childhood education. *Phi Delta Kappan, 85*(5), 388–396.

Kauerz, K., & Coffman, J. (2013). *Framework for planning, implementing and evaluating preK–3rd grade approaches.* Seattle, WA: College of Education, University of Washington.

Lahti, M., Sabol, T., Starr, R., Langill, C., & Tout, K. (2013). *Validation of quality rating and improvement systems (QRIS): Examples from four states.* Research-to-Practice Brief OPRE 2013-036. Washington, DC: Office of Planning, Research and Evaluation, Administration for Children and Families, U.S. Department of Health and Human Services.

Mead, S. (2009). *Education reform starts early: Lessons from New Jersey's preK–3rd reform efforts.* Washington, DC: New America Foundation.

Mead, S. (2013, August 28). Do QRIS improve student outcomes? *Education Week.* Retrieved from http://blogs.edweek.org/edweek/sarameads_policy_notebook/2013/08/do_qris_improve_student_outcomes.html

Meisels, S. J. (2006). Accountability in early childhood: No easy answers. *Herr Research Center for Children and Social Policy, Erikson Institute.* Retrieved from www.isbe.state.il.us/earlychi/pdf/meisels_accountability.pdf

Mitchell, A. (2009). *Quality rating and improvement systems as a framework for early care and education system reform.* Boston, MA: BUILD Initiative.

National Early Childhood Accountability Task Force. (2007). *Taking stock: Assessing and improving early childhood learning and program quality.* Washington, DC: Pew Center on the States: Author.

Regenstein, E., & Lipper, K. (2013). *A framework for choosing a state-level early childhood governance system.* Denver, CO: BUILD Initiative. Retrieved from www.buildinitiative.org/Portals/0/Uploads/Documents/Early%20Childhood%20Governance%20for%20Web.pdf

Regenstein, E., & Romero-Jurado, R. (2014). *A framework for rethinking education accountability and support birth through high school.* Chicago, IL: Ounce of Prevention Fund.

Schultz, T. (2008). Tackling pk–3 assessment and accountability challenges: Guidance from the National Early Childhood Accountability Task Force. *The State Education Standard* (June), 4–11.

Schultz, T. (2014). *Evaluating preK-3rd school district, state and federal policy factors.* New York, NY: Foundation for Child Development.

Scott-Little, C., Kagan, S. L., Frelow, V. S., & Reid, J. (2009). Infant-toddler early learning guidelines: The content that states have addressed and implications for programs serving children with disabilities. *Infants and Young Children, 22*(2), 87–99.

Snow, C. E., & Van Hemel, S. (Eds.) (2008). *Early childhood assessment: Why, what, and how.* Committee on Developmental Outcomes and Assessments for Young Children, Board on Children, Youth and Families, Board on Testing and Assessment, Division of Behavioral and Social Sciences and Education. Washington, DC: National Academies Press.

Tout, K., Halle, T., Daily, S., Albertson-Junkans, L., & Moodie, S. (2013). *The research base for a birth through age eight state policy framework.* Bethesda, MD: Child Trends. Retrieved from http://earlysuccess.org/sites/default/files/website_files/files/B8%20Policy%20Framework%20Research.pdf

Tout, K., Starr, R., Soli, M., Moodie, S., Kirby, G., & Boller, K. (2010). *Compendium of quality rating and improvement systems.* Washington, DC: Child Trends.

Tout, K., Zaslow, M., Halle, T., & Forry, N. (2009). *Issues for the next decade of quality rating and improvement systems.* Washington, DC: Child Trends.

U.S. Department of Education. (2013). *Race to the Top—Early learning challenge.* Washington, DC: Office of Early Learning. Retrieved from www2.ed.gov/programs/racetothetop-earlylearningchallenge/index.html.

U.S. Department of Health and Human Services. (2009). *Head Start program performance standards 45 CFR Chapter XIII.* Washington, DC: Administration for Children and Families. Retrieved from http://eclkc.ohs.acf.hhs.gov/hslc/standards/Head%20Start%20Requirements/45%20CFR%20Chapter%20XIII/45%20CFR%20Chap%20XIII_ENG.pdf

U.S. Department of Health and Human Services. (2010a). *The Head Start Child Development and Early Learning Framework: Promoting positive outcomes in early childhood programs serving children 3–5 years old.* Washington, DC: Administration on Children, Youth and Families.

U.S. Department of Health and Human Services. (2010b). *Designation renewal of Head Start grantees.* Federal Register, 75, no. 183: 57704. Washington, DC: Administration on Children and Families. Retrieved from www.gpo.gov/fdsys/pkg/FR-2010-09-22/pdf/2010-23583.pdf

Wallen, M., & Hubbard, A. (2013). *Blending and braiding early childhood program funding streams toolkit.* Chicago, IL: Ounce of Prevention Fund.

Zellman, G., & Karoly, L. (2012). *Moving to outcomes: Approaches to incorporating child assessments into state early childhood quality rating and improvement systems.* Santa Monica, CA: RAND Corporation. Retrieved from www.rand.org/pubs/occasional_papers/OP364.html

CHAPTER 8

Early Childhood Data Governance
A Prerequisite for Answering Important Policy Questions

Missy Cochenour and Kathleen Hebbeler

> *Scenario 1:* The lieutenant governor's office wants to know how many children in the state's pre-K program are receiving subsidized child care.
>
> *Scenario 2:* The director of the Department of Health's early intervention program for infants and toddlers with disabilities wants to know how many early intervention recipients are found eligible for preschool special education as 4-year-olds.
>
> *Scenario 3:* A researcher wants to compare the kindergarten entry assessment scores of children who attended Head Start with those who did not.

The common theme across the preceding scenarios is that each requires linking data across more than one of the state's early childhood programs. As states move to build a more comprehensive and integrated system of programs for young children and their families, they also are moving to build data systems that contain data from multiple programs such as Head Start and Early Head Start, state preschool and child-care programs, and preschool special education and early intervention for infants and toddlers with disabilities. There is widespread recognition of the importance of having good data on early childhood programs and the need for linked data across programs (ECDC, 2010; Hernandez, 2012; OECD, 2012; UNESCO, 2002). Many states that are moving toward more unified forms of early childhood governance also are developing integrated data systems to support their vision of an improved system of services for children and their families (ECDC, 2014). The states that have chosen to pursue linking data across programs will need to institute a special form of governance, data governance, to oversee the planning and management of their new integrated data systems.

This chapter examines the critical role that data governance plays in supporting overall early childhood governance in building an integrated data system. It provides an overview of key concepts in early childhood data governance including what it is, its relationship to overall early childhood governance, how it is structured, the stages of good data governance, and where states are in establishing data governance.

DEFINING DATA GOVERNANCE

In business, data are seen as an asset that needs to be both managed and protected (Redman, 2008). The education and the human services sectors increasingly are coming to this same realization. As part of its support to states in developing longitudinal data systems, the National Center for Education Statistics (NCES) defined data governance specific to education: "[It] is both an organizational process and a structure; it establishes responsibility for data, organizing program area staff to collaboratively and continuously improve data quality through the systematic creation and enforcement of policies, roles, responsibilities, and procedures" (National Forum on Education Statistics, 2011, p. 9). The NCES definition, which is used in this chapter, also is used by technical assistance providers working with states to develop integrated data systems. The authors of this chapter work with these technical assistance efforts and will draw on the materials from these projects and their experiences with states throughout this chapter.

This chapter addresses the type of data governance needed to establish and maintain a data system that links data across early childhood programs. Referred to as an Early Childhood Integrated Data System (ECIDS), this type of data system "collects, integrates, maintains, stores, and reports information from early childhood programs across multiple agencies within a state that serve children and families from birth to age eight" (Cochenour, Chatis, Irvine, Sellers, & Duarte, 2014, p. 1).

Data governance supports, but is distinct from, overall early childhood education (ECE) governance. Overall, ECE governance refers to the structures and functions through which early childhood services are managed, implemented, and held accountable. It oversees the entire scope of the state's early childhood initiatives, whereas data governance focuses specifically on decisions related to the data elements, data access, data standards, quality, privacy, security, and use. Yet ECE governance plays an essential role with regard to data: It helps determine information priorities and identifies the leadership and program area staff that will participate from each agency or program. Typically, the decision of whether to pursue the linking of data across programs would be made by a state's overall early childhood governance.

WHY IS DATA GOVERNANCE NECESSARY?

Data governance is necessary because managing data policies and procedures goes beyond the scope of the overall early childhood governance body. Agency leaders are likely to lack knowledge about the nuances of each program's data as well as the implications if changes were to be made to the way a particular data element is collected. Developing and sustaining an ECIDS is an extremely complex undertaking that presents numerous programmatic and technical challenges. Addressing these challenges requires that agency leadership and staff work collaboratively with IT staff through a data governance structure to ensure good communication for decision-making and appropriate levels of involvement of the various parties.

The need for data governance exists whether or not the state has consolidated overall early childhood governance into a single agency because individual programs typically have their own data systems, sometimes extending back many years. Creating a single early childhood agency in the state does not automatically create an ECIDS. A consolidated ECE governance structure facilitates the development of an ECIDS, but data governance is still required to ensure that the new integrated system will address each program's unique demand for information, including addressing any federal reporting requirements. Data governance also provides the structure for including data from any early childhood programs that fall outside the authority of a more consolidated governance structure.

Although states have established early childhood data governance without overall governance in place, ideally, an overall governance body provides the leadership support to establish the data governance structure. The success and sustainability of early childhood data governance requires the support of those who govern early childhood in the state.

PRINCIPLES AND STRUCTURE

Effective data governance for an ECIDS is founded on three central principles:

- *All* agencies and programs contributing early childhood information to the system are represented at the leadership and implementation levels. No agency should be expected to contribute information without being represented in the decisionmaking.
- Program areas, IT, and leadership hold distinct roles and decisionmaking authority, and clear relationships exist among their roles. Data governance is not an IT initiative.
- Agencies and programs establish common data definitions, operating procedures, and processes for managing the ECIDS data (Cochenour, Chatis, & Irvine, 2014).

Although this chapter focuses on data governance across early childhood agencies and programs, it is important to note that the individual programs contributing data to a state's ECIDS have already established some form of data governance *within* their individual programs to address many of the same issues for their own program data. Early childhood programs with strong program-level governance will be able to leverage the lessons learned to support the development of data governance for an integrated data system.

States' experiences in developing statewide longitudinal data systems, also an interagency effort, indicate that a multilayered structure with well-defined roles and responsibilities for each layer is needed for data governance. An effective data governance structure includes a data governance coordinator and three critical groups: (1) a Data Policy Committee, (2) a Data Management Committee, and (3) a Data Stewards Committee, with IT personnel embedded throughout. Participants in these groups should have the authority to make the key decisions outlined for the work and understand when to escalate an issue to another group in the data governance structure (see Figure 8.1) (Cochenour, Chatis, & Irvine, 2014).

Each group has different members and unique responsibilities. The Data Policy Committee is made up of the executive leaders from each program or agency contributing data to the ECIDS and may include some of the same individuals serving on an overall early childhood governance group. This overlap ensures that there is the leadership support and direction needed for data decisions to be made across agencies. The Data Policy Committee is responsible for establishing the state goals, policies, and direction for the ECIDS and for communicating with overall early childhood governance.

The next level of data governance, the Data Management Committee, consists of the managers or directors of all programs that contribute data to the ECIDS. This level establishes and documents interagency program standards for data collection, reporting, and the release of data needed to support addressing the state's essential policy and programmatic questions.

Figure 8.1. A Structure for Early Childhood Data Governance

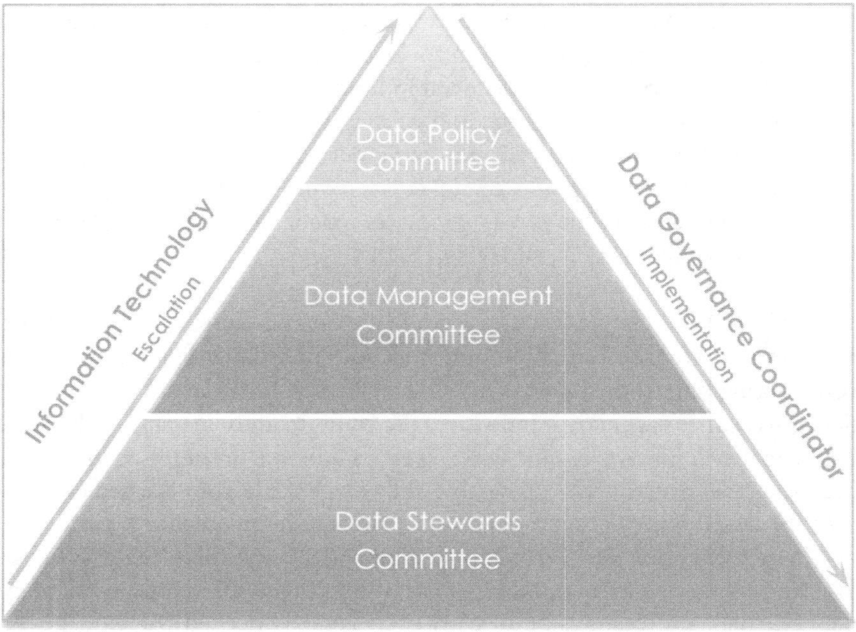

The Data Stewards, the next level of data governance, are the members of the program staff who are knowledgeable about the data elements and the program requirements for data collection. They are responsible for determining the data elements and business rules necessary to answer the essential questions and to resolve critical data issues within the program area.

The data governance coordinator ensures that the layers of the data governance structure work in concert with one another. The data governance coordinator is a member of each committee and is also responsible for connecting the work and decisions, from escalation through implementation, among the groups. This individual is an essential component of the data governance structure, ensuring the consistency and flow of information between groups and allowing for coordination among groups without the need for additional meetings of the entire body. External stakeholders, such as researchers, may serve in an advisory role, but only those directly responsible for managing the data and setting policies around its collection and use should be involved in data governance.

STAGES OF EARLY CHILDHOOD DATA GOVERNANCE

Data governance is developed over time in a state. Some states begin moving toward formal data governance by establishing an advisory body within overall governance that might later evolve into a formal data governance structure. This advisory body could be, for example, a subcommittee of the state's early childhood advisory committee that is charged with determining the data needs of the state. The political and technical challenges that must be addressed in the development of an ECIDS require a data governance structure that is considerably more intricate than a data subcommittee to the overall governance body. A subcommittee has limited responsibilities and is not data governance, but is a preliminary step toward the development of formal early childhood data governance.

The three stages of data governance are *establishing*, *implementing*, and *improving*. In the establishing phase, states identify the agency and program partners that will be data contributors and work with executive leadership to assign the appropriate staff with the authority to make decisions (Cochenour, Chatis, & Irvine, 2014). Once states have established data governance, they begin to implement their processes and make decisions as a body related to the integrated data system. In this stage, states operationalize their data governance plans to make decisions around the scope, integration, refresh, changes, access, requests, and releases (Cochenour, Chatis, & Irvine, 2014). Examples of decisions made at this stage include: (1) how often and how data will be updated, (2) who will have what level of access to the ECIDS, and (3) how reports and other data products will be identified, produced, and released. The lessons learned through these decisions lead to the final stage: continuous improvement of early childhood data governance. Data governance is not created once and then maintained. Continuous improvement includes activities such as reviewing how well the policies and procedures are working. By this stage, the state has established the structure and processes necessary to proactively identify and prevent problems in data quality, use, or privacy. In addition, agency leadership and staff are now working collaboratively with IT staff through a data governance structure to ensure good communication for decisionmaking and appropriate levels of involvement among the various parties. This advanced stage of data governance increases the state's odds of being able to navigate the many challenges of building and maintaining an integrated data system.

An example of how good data governance improves data quality and reduces data burden comes from a state that struggled to correctly capture the ages of children served by multiple programs. Data governance is responsible for ensuring that what appear to be the same data elements across programs are truly the same (Chang, 2012). For years, the state maintained that there was duplicate and erroneous reporting of age data across programs. When the state examined the age of the same child being served by multiple programs, it found inconsistencies with the child being a 1-year-old for one program but a 2-year-old for another. The inconsistencies resulted from the programs using different points of time to calculate the child's age. One program used age as of December 1 for reporting child count and the other collected age at the beginning of the school year. The state was able to solve this problem because the governance body provided a mechanism to allow a detailed look at how the programs were collecting age data. Although this was not a difficult problem to solve, it did require agencies to compare their procedures for data collection; data governance provided the forum for the examination and the resolution.

States have been making progress in recent years toward the development of an ECIDS, with some establishing committees to address data issues and others moving toward formal data governance. According to the 2013 Early Childhood Data Collaborative survey, only one state, Pennsylvania, reports being able to link data across multiple early childhood programs (ECDC, 2014), but 32 states reported that their state had designated a lead agency or a cross-department entity as the state's early childhood data governance body. Eleven states were planning to establish a data governance body, and eight states indicated that they had no entity designated for data governance (ECDC, 2014). A survey that looked exclusively at the state agencies focused on young children with disabilities found that 14 states had a data governance body that included the Part C early intervention program, and 37 had a data governance body that included preschool special education (Derrington, Spiker, Hebbeler, & Diefendorf, 2013).

Clearly, states still have much work to do in establishing the data governance structures and processes that are needed to support data sharing across early childhood programs.

CONCLUSIONS

The nature of the relationship of data governance to overall early childhood governance varies across states, but the best available information suggests that overall early childhood governance bodies that strategically establish the necessary structure and processes for good data governance significantly increase the state's odds of being able to navigate the many challenges of building and maintaining an integrated data system.

Effective data governance provides many benefits for a state's early childhood system. First and foremost, early childhood data governance supports overall early childhood governance by providing valuable information. By maximizing the return on the state's data investments, data governance provides early childhood governance with the credibility, visibility, and authority associated with responsible, data-informed decisions. Additional benefits of data governance include improved communication among program staff and between program staff and IT, which produces a more cost-effective technical solution for the state's ECIDs; appropriate and secure sharing of data across early childhood programs; and finally, improved data quality and use that results from a better understanding of how each program collects its data and what those data mean.

Access to good information is a critical tool for states to make improvements and bolster public support for early childhood services and programs. States need to be able to formulate and address a range of programmatic and policy questions about the children receiving services; the quantity, quality, and cost of what they are receiving; and the outcomes and benefits to children and their families. As states move to build more consolidated systems of overall early childhood governance, they also need to lay the groundwork for collecting, storing, sharing, and using high-quality data. Data represent an asset whose value is maximized when information about children and programs can be examined across programs and across time. Although states face numerous challenges in developing integrated early childhood data systems, many of these challenges can be addressed with data governance. Effective data governance provides overall early childhood governance with the structure and processes to produce better information to implement cross-agency improvements and to demonstrate the return on their investments in early childhood.

NOTE

The federal Statewide Longitudinal Data System (SLDS) Grant program currently offers technical assistance to states working on their ECIDS as a foundation for the longitudinal data system efforts within each state (https://nces.ed.gov/programs/slds/index.asp). Within special education, a technical assistance center supports early intervention and early childhood special education state programs funded under the IDEA in improving the quality of their data and supporting their participation in their states ECIDS (http://dasycenter.org/). Additionally, states that have received Race to the Top Early Learning Challenge Grants (RTT–ELC) are provided with technical assistance to develop their ECIDS.

REFERENCES

Chang, M. Y. (2012). *Recommendations for developing a unified early childhood data system*. Lincoln, NE: Nebraska Department of Education for the Early Childhood Interagency Coordinating Council.

Cochenour, M., Chatis, C., & Irvine, S. (2014). *Early childhood data governance in action: An introduction*. Washington, DC: National Center for Education Statistics, Institute of Education Sciences, U.S. Department of Education.

Cochenour, M., Chatis, C., Irvine, S., Sellers, J., & Duarte, S. (2014). *What is an early childhood integrated data system?* Washington, DC: National Center for Education Statistics, Institute of Education Sciences, U.S. Department of Education.

Derrington, T., Spiker, D., Hebbeler, K., & Diefendorf, M. (2013). *IDEA Part C and Part B 619 state data systems: Current status and future priorities*. Menlo Park, CA: SRI International. Retrieved from www.dasycenter.org/resources/papers/dasy-needs-assessment-report.html

Early Childhood Data Collaborative (ECDC). (2010). *Building and using coordinated state early care and education data systems. A framework for state policymakers*. Washington, DC: Author. Retrieved from www.ecedata.org/files/Building%20and%20Using%20Coordinated%20State%20Early%20Care%20and%20Education%20Data%20Systems.pdf

Early Childhood Data Collaborative (ECDC). (2014). *2013 state of states' early childhood data systems* (2014-06). Retrieved from www.ecedata.org/files/2013%20State%20of%20States%27%20Early%20Childhood%20Data%20Systems.pdf

Hernandez, D. F. (2012). *PreK–3rd: Next steps for state longitudinal data systems* (PreK–3rd Policy to Action Brief No. Eight). New York, NY: Foundation for Child Development. Retrieved from http://fcd-us.org/sites/default/files/Next%20Steps%20for%20State%20Longitudinal%20Data%20Systems_0.pdf

National Forum on Education Statistics. (2011). *Traveling through time: The forum guide to longitudinal data system. Book three of four: Effectively managing LDS data* (NFES 2011–805) (NFES 2001-805). Washington, DC: National Center for Education Statistics, Institute of Education Sciences, U.S. Department of Education. Retrieved from http://nces.ed.gov/forum/pub_2011805.asp

Organisation for Economic Co-operation and Development (OECD). (2012). *Starting strong III: A quality toolbox for early childhood education and care*. Paris, France: OECD Publishing. Retrieved from http://dx.doi.org/10.1787/9789264123564-en

Redman, T. C. (2008). *Data driven: Profiting from your most important business asset*. Boston, MA: Harvard Business School.

United Nations Educational, Scientific, and Cultural Organisation (UNESCO). (2002). *Planning for access: Develop a data system first* (UNESCO Policy Brief on Early Childhood No. 2). Paris, France: Section for Early Childhood and Inclusive Education, UNESCO. Retrieved from http://unesdoc.unesco.org/ulis/cgi-bin/ulis.pl?catno=137376&set=530BB31E_2_420&gp=1&mode=e&lin=1&ll=1

CHAPTER 9

Governance and Financing

Rolf Grafwallner

A stable and sustainable financing strategy is key for early childhood systems development. Governance, as a key element in systems development, has, in some states, influenced revenue generation, distribution, and expansion in ways that enhance services, reduce their duplication, and increase financial accountability. Additionally, states have used governance as a lever to examine and experiment with new approaches to financing. This chapter explores the link between governance and financing mechanisms—traditional and innovative—for early childhood education.

TRADITIONAL PUBLIC FINANCING OF ECE

Traditional public funding for early childhood education comes through federal, state, and local sources. Federal investment is linked to national legislation, such as funds for child-care subsidy or for children with disabilities. State funding is driven by enhancing federal funds such as funding for infants and toddlers with disabilities or by signature state initiatives such as preschool education. Local sources are typically characterized as supplementing federal or state initiatives.

Federal Funding

Federal funding in early childhood education programs is administered through 45 programs that provide or support services to children ages birth to 5 (U.S. General Accounting Office [GAO], 2014).

Conventional public financing of early childhood education programs for all 50 states and territories is designed to support the implementation of mandated programs. Table 9.1 lists the most common federal funding resources and their purposes.

Table 9.1. Most Common Federal Funding Resources by Purpose and Authorization

Federal Funding Source	Purpose	Authorization
Child Care and Development Fund (CCDF)	Provision of child-care subsidy and quality improvements in child care	Child Care and Development Block Grant (CCDBG)
Temporary Assistance for Needy Families (TANF)	Assistance to low-income families, including child care	Personal Responsibility and Work Opportunity Act of 1996
Child and Adult Care Food Program (CACFP)	Provision of meal reimbursement and nutrition education	National School Lunch Act, Section 17
Section 619 and Part C (preschool special education and infants and toddlers programs)	Provision of services for children with disabilities, birth to 21 years. Section 619 and Part C (of the law) provides funds for child with disabilities, birth to age 6	Individuals with Disabilities Education Act (IDEA)
Head Start and Early Head Start	Provision of services for low-income children, birth to age 5. Funding bypasses state governments	Head Start Act of 1965
Title I	Provision of educational services for disadvantaged children (prekindergarten to grade 12)	Elementary and Secondary Education Act (ESEA)
Maternal, Infant, and Early Childhood Home Visiting Program	Provision for maternal and newborn health and positive child outcomes through evidence-based home visiting	Social Security Act, Title V (amended by the Patient Protection and Affordable Care Act)

Although all these federal funding sources appropriate funding for divergent purposes, state governments can use them flexibly as long as the main function of the funds is met. Among the resources listed in Table 9.1, the least restrictive are the CCDF and TANF. For instance, as long as 70% of CCDF funds are spent on child-care subsidy, and at least 4% of the funds are spent on quality improvements in child care, states have the flexibility to apply the funds to meet the strategic benchmarks of their state plans (U.S. Department of Health and Human Services, 2012). The TANF grants are even more flexible than the CCDF block grants. Many states consider TANF grants state funds to be used for mandatory programs, such as foster care and targeted cash assistance (TCA) for eligible low-income families where an adult in the family is in school or at work. Up to 30% of the state's TANF grant can be earmarked for child care, either for direct subsidies or for quality improvement. If a state uses TANF funds for a child-care subsidy or for quality improvements, the rules of the CCDF apply (Center for Law and Social Policy, 2010).

More restrictive than the CCDF or TANF are the CACFP and the Section 619 and Part C portions of the Individuals with Disabilities Education Act (IDEA). Meal reimbursement funds of the CACFP must be spent on meals in compliance with federal nutrition guidelines. The CACFP allows for costs to administer the program, which, at a larger scale, enables child-care operators to promote nutrition education in their programs. Part C and Section 619 funds under IDEA must be used to improve outcomes for young children with disabilities. Although the disbursement of IDEA funds follows state policies regarding services for young children with disabilities, federal procedures impose safeguards for implementation. Built into IDEA, these safeguards ensure consistency and clear expectations for families of children with disabilities.

Head Start and Early Start, on the other hand, are highly restrictive programs, as a result of the federal government's desire to ensure that local communities and local school districts use the funding to benefit disadvantaged children. Originally dubbed a compensatory program, Head Start has become a critical funding source for the country's community-based organizations and local school districts. State government takes a back seat to imprinting its political will on these programs, with the exception of dedicated funds for Head Start Collaboration. The only control that states exercise in terms of Head Start funds is their ability to influence local decisionmakers to consolidate or coordinate Head Start programs with public school prekindergarten or local child-care programs. A consolidated governance model exerts such influence primarily through its direct funding authority over child-care and prekindergarten funds.

State and Local Funding

Aside from matching federal funds, state and local governments have increasingly become benefactors of early childhood programs. Nowhere is this more evident than in states' aggressive investments in preschool education and full-day kindergarten during the past 10 years (Barnett, Carolan, Fitzgerald, & Squires, 2012; Children's Defense Fund, 2012). Table 9.2 lists the states' prekindergarten, kindergarten, and early intervention funds by purpose and oversight.

The past decade has seen states become significant players in defining the mission of early childhood education. While federal funds focused on child care, women's access to the workforce, and addressing inequality of

Table 9.2. State and Local Fund Sources by Purpose and Authorization

State and Local Fund Source	Purpose	Authorization
Prekindergarten	High-quality educational services for 3- and 4-year-olds either targeted to low-income children or universal	State legislation or governor's budget
Full-Day Kindergarten	Extended kindergarten program for 5-year-olds either targeted to low-income communities or universal	State legislation or local school district policies
Early Intervention Services	Provision of services for children with disabilities by supplementing Federal Section 619 or Part C funds	State legislation, governor's budget, or local school district policies
Head Start (Supplemental Funds)	Provision of Head Start services (see Table 9.1) or specialized services (e.g., extended hours of service or summer programs) for Head Start children	State legislation or governor's budget

access to educational services for minority children and children with disabilities, the state and local school districts' main function of early childhood education has focused on young children's readiness for school. A huge proliferation of prekindergarten programs funded by state legislatures, budget allocations by governors, or local property taxes reflects a growing understanding among state policymakers and school administrators that upfront investments in young children's early education might save remediation costs later in K–12 education (ReadyNation, 2013).

Such increased state investments not only complicate the purposes or missions of early childhood education, but also prompt significant challenges to the already highly fragmented early childhood education state governance structure. Fueled by increased state investments, the merging of agencies was regarded by key decisionmakers as a potential remedy for resolving the fragmentation.

GOVERNANCE AS A STRATEGY FOR FINANCE REFORM IN ECE

Starting around 2000, many states began to look at ways to reform the governance structure of early childhood programs. Hampered in the past by the inefficiencies of working across multiple agencies with diverse missions, often functioning at cross-purposes, and urged by an increasing focus on aligning education, policymakers are now striving to create more consistent and efficient ways to govern early childhood education (Regenstein & Lipper, 2013). The consolidation of conventional early care and education funding into one major agency is often at the heart of such efforts. Consolidation takes many forms. For example, Pennsylvania established the Office of Child Development and Early Learning (OCDEL) in 2006 through an executive order. This governance approach combines funding and staff from the state's Departments of Education and Public Welfare to coordinate early care and education services. Other states, such as California, are consolidating services for young children in state departments of education (Regenstein & Lipper, 2013). Taking a similar approach and using legislative fiat, Maryland transferred all its early childhood programs into the state Department of Education in 2005 and 2006. In so doing, the state also created a new Division of Early Childhood Development and an executive-level position to head it, thereby elevating the role of early childhood education in the state's education reform efforts (Maryland State Department of Education, 2007). In 2011, Michigan created the Office of Great Start, consolidating early education programs within the state Department of Education. These states exemplify the new trend of linking early childhood education with K–12 education reform, with the goals of not only overseeing all of the critical programs, but also of consolidating budget decisions for all federal and state resources for early childhood education.

Such consolidated governance has allowed for strategic opportunities that were unheard of just 10 years ago. Concepts such as "braided" and "blended funding," once only theoretical ideas, have become practical realities (Ounce of Prevention, 2013). With prekindergarten, child-care, early intervention, and other early childhood education funds at the disposal of one agency, the development and implementation of a coherent and coordinated strategic plan to boost young children's learning and school readiness skills can be realized. In contrast to the prior governance approach, when critical budgetary or fiscal decisions had to be supported by two or three different agency heads, the new structures allow for a more direct execution of decisionmaking, thereby speeding up initiatives and clarifying the accountable entities to the public.

Governance reform in Maryland and Michigan did not categorically impact finance reform, such as extending formula-based public aid to early childhood education. But it reformed the way the consolidated agencies used federal and state funding, which used to be in different agencies, and applied it more strategically to meet specific agency goals. In both states, the consolidated fund resources have become the centerpiece for improving the infrastructure and the conditions of early learning for the whole population of young children. The process of consolidation also gave credence and accountability to a system that has been handicapped by fragmentation and a lack of focus for decades. By consolidating all programs within one agency, policymakers were well positioned to initiate bold reforms and react to comprehensive federal education initiatives, such as the Race to the Top–Early Learning Challenge Fund. For example, in 2011, four out of the nine winning states developed their state plans from a consolidated state governance platform—California, Massachusetts, Maryland, and Washington. Michigan also publicly announced governance consolidation as a means to increase its competitiveness in the RTT competition (Snyder, 2011). By upgrading the organizational stature within an agency or by creating a new consolidated agency, the budgetary review process within an administration and by the legislature takes on more significance. For instance, Maryland's Division of Early Childhood Development within the state Department of Education has its own annual budget analysis and hearing, including accountability benchmarks for early childhood education (Maryland Department of Legislative Services, 2014).

An oft-cited rationale for consolidating governance is that it allows funds to be used more efficiently. This argument, mostly touted by legislatures or governors as a way to bring government reform in alignment with budgetary targets, has proven to be more complicated than anticipated. Both Maryland and Michigan report that additional funds had to be requested and approved to implement the startup costs for the governance reform (Esther Lindy Buch, personal communication, November 4, 2013; Maryland Department of Legislative Services, 2014). Both states, however, also observed that governance reform reduced the scope of redundancies of services, such as technology support or the provision of a comprehensive professional development program with customization for disparate constituencies (e.g., public school teachers or family child-care providers).

NEW FRONTIERS FOR FINANCING ECE: FOUNDATIONS AND VENTURE CAPITAL

Consolidated governance cannot claim sole credit for the emergence of new approaches to financing in early childhood education. It can, however, lay claim to fostering greater fiscal attention to early childhood, leading to a reconceptualization of the government's role as the key financer of early education. Interestingly, as part of a mobilization of private resources for social and educational purposes, an increasing number of venture capitalists have expressed interest in investing in early childhood education (Chamber of Commerce, 2010; ReadyNation, 2013). In fact, according to Salamon

(2014), a "significant revolution appears to be underway of the frontiers of philanthropy." (p. 4) Where in the past support was provided through donations, gifts, and foundation grants, now "a bewildering array of new instruments and institutions has surfaced" (Salamon, 2014, p. 4). Instruments that have been used in the financial markets are now being introduced for social investments, including early childhood education. Such instruments are loans and loan guarantees, equity-type investments, or social impact bonds. For instance, a small foundation in Baltimore serves as the broker for financing the operation of early childhood projects. A host of new actors—venture capitalists, corporations, and individual donors—invest in long-term outcomes by establishing agreements with the state and the local school system to operate research-based and proven early childhood partnerships.

The two main underlying principles of the new investment tools are creating incentives for providers to achieve better outcomes at lower costs, and for the foundations to save money as a result of the cost efficiencies. Early childhood education, with its potential long-term savings, has frequently been mentioned as a prime candidate for the new financing tools (Agency for Healthcare Research and Quality, 2012; Dugger, 2013).

The new wave of investment opportunities for early childhood education is connected to the trend toward consolidated governance. If consolidated governance spurs greater transparency and accountability, then investors in human capital can see less vulnerability and lower risk for their capital investments. Clear evidence about these new investment strategies is still emerging, however. The implementation of the new investment tools, as applied to early childhood education, is so current that only one project exists countrywide. (The United Way of Salt Lake City uses investment from Goldman Sachs and the J. B. Pritzker Foundation to operate the Utah High Quality Preschool Program.) Yet, this surge in innovative approaches to financing cannot be dismissed. Ultimately the success of these efforts may well be linked to the degree that early education is organized, streamlined, and cost-effective as a system, facts made more feasible when governance is consolidated.

CONCLUSIONS

The consolidation of funding streams in support of early education services has coincided with the emergence of new governance models to create improved statewide systems of early childhood education. Bringing the oversight of all early childhood programs "under one roof" has brought improved coordination, coherence, and accountability to programs and how they are being funded (Regenstein & Lipper, 2013). Although the degree of restrictiveness among some funding sources (e.g., IDEA, Head Start) does not easily lend itself to a blending of funding, less restrictive funding sources (i.e., CCDF) can be shaped to support or connect mandatory services that were disparate and disconnected from one another. Early childhood education, as a developing professional field, warrants greater public investment. But under the constraints of current budgetary policies, the most valuable option for further growth lies in the integration of public funding and private investment. Though it is still in its infancy, private investment in early education will not only challenge the system to produce socially beneficial outcomes, but it will also broaden the scope and importance of early childhood education as a viable candidate in human capital investment.

REFERENCES

Agency for Healthcare Research and Quality. (2012). *Pay for performance (P4P): AHRQ Resources.* Retrieved from www.ahrq.gov/professionals/quality-patient -safety/quality-resources/tools/pay4per/index.html

Barnett, W. S., Carolan, M. E., Fitzgerald, J., & Squires, J. H. (2012). *The state of preschool 2012: State preschool yearbook.* New Brunswick, NJ: National Institute for Early Education Research. Retrieved from http://nieer.org/sites/ nieer/files/yearbook2012.pdf

Center for Law and Social Policy. (2010). *Child care assistance profile.* Retrieved from www.clasp.org/resources-and-publications/files/2010-Child-Care-Assistance -Profile-US.pdf

Chamber of Commerce. (2010). *Why business should support early childhood education.* Retrieved from http://education.uschamber.com/sites/default/files/ICW_ EarlyChildhoodReport_2010.pdf

Children's Defense Fund. (2012). *Increasing access to full-day K.* Retrieved from www.childrensdefense.org/child-research-data-publications/data/increasing-access-full-day-k.pdf

Dugger, R. (2013). Early childhood human capital investment: "Pay for success" finance. In D. S. Harburger, M. Zabel, R. Tsakalas, J. V. Spears, R. H. Grafwallner, and Social Impact Workgroup (Eds.), *Social impact bonds in Maryland* (pp. 83–116). Report to the Maryland General Assembly, House Appropriations Committee. Baltimore, MD: Maryland State Department of Education.

Maryland Department of Legislative Services. (2014). *Analysis of the FY2015 Maryland Executive Budget.* Retrieved from http://mgaleg.maryland.gov/pubs/ budgetfiscal/2015fy-budget-docs-operating-R00A99-MSDE-Early-Childhood-Development.pdf

Maryland State Department of Education. (2007). *Maryland educational initiatives.* Retrieved from www.marylandpublicschools.org/NR/rdonlyres/50E778B3-88E6-4276-8CA4-981A50B7F31D/13840/eli_final.pdf

Ounce of Prevention. (2013). *Blending and braiding early childhood program funding streams toolkit.* Retrieved from www.ounceofprevention.org/national-policy /Blended-Funding-Toolkit-Nov2013.pdf

ReadyNation (Producer). (2013). *Early childhood is serious business: A conversation with executives* [video]. Retrieved from www.readynation.org/summit2013

Regenstein, E., & Lipper, K. (2013). *A framework for choosing a state-level early childhood governance system.* Retrieved from www.buildinitiative.org/ Portals/0/Uploads/Documents/Early%20Childhood%20Governance%20 for%20Web.pdf

Salamon, L. M. (2014). The revolution on the frontiers of philanthropy: An introduction. In L. M. Salamon (Ed.), *The frontiers of philanthropy* (pp. 3–87). New York, NY: Oxford University Press..

Snyder, R. (2011). Michigan State Executive Order 2011-8 (June 29, 2011).

U.S. Department of Health and Human Services, Administration of Children and Youth. (2012). *Fact sheet: Child care and development fund.* Retrieved from www.acf.hhs.gov/programs/occ/fact-sheet-occ

U.S. General Accounting Office. (2014). *Early learning and child care: Federal funds support multiple programs with similar goals.* Retrieved from www.gao.gov/ assets/670/660685.pdf

CHAPTER 10

Governance and Professional Development Systems

Sarah LeMoine

Early childhood and school-age professional development (PD) systems link and provide training, formal education, technical assistance, and related services and supports. PD systems help the potential and current workforce to: (1) understand what PD is available; (2) access it, complete it, and apply new knowledge and skills in their work; and (3) advance their careers. A PD system is a subset of the overall early childhood education system.

The governance of early childhood education, as this volume clearly indicates, is both complex and evolving. As a subsystem, PD systems are impacted by the overall early childhood education system governance. This chapter explores the relationships among state/territory early childhood education system governance, PD system governance, and approaches to PD system administration. States/territories are expanding their early childhood/school-age system vision to include multiple settings and sectors. Their expanded vision conveys the message that the early childhood/school-age system serves "one set" of young children and consequently that there is *one workforce* that serves these children and their families. In response to this expanded vision and encouraged by related federal and state programs, governance structures are emerging that model and support integrated systems. A PD system's governance affects the way in which its core services are designed and delivered. One of the most important decisions governing bodies influence is PD system administration, including which entity implements the system and the design of service delivery.

VISION AND GOVERNANCE

Over the past decade, there has been a significant increase in reorganization of states' early childhood education systems governance. Whatever a state's exact governance approach is, the professional development for the ECE workforce in that state remains a central focus and a critical element. In most states, the early childhood education governance entity develops a committee, subcommittee, or similar work group that defines a vision and goals for its PD system that complements the overall early childhood/school-age system vision and priorities.

PD system's governance and administration is closely tied to the state's priorities for the workforce (see Figure 10.1). The vision for a PD system articulates its foundation, the focus of its functions, and its place in the early childhood education system. Both the system's governing body and its articulated vision for the system influence the PD system's administration.

Expanding System Vision

Before the turn of this century, most state PD systems focused primarily on the child-care workforce because, unlike Head Start and P–12 public education, this sector did not have an institutionalized infrastructure for PD. Today, however, most state PD system vision statements articulate an intent to serve everyone who works with or on behalf of young children (and sometimes school-age children and youth).

Several key federal programs support this broadened vision and encourage states to build and implement cross-sector, integrated PD systems. For example, the State Advisory Councils for Early Care and Education, part of the Head Start Act reauthorization of 2007, emphasize the role of integrated PD systems and institutes of higher education (IHEs) in building

Figure 10.1. Governance, Vision, and Administration

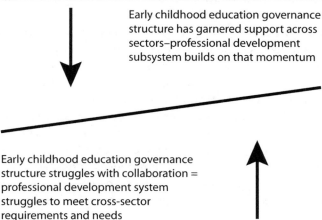

Early childhood education governance structure has garnered support across sectors–professional development subsystem builds on that momentum

Early childhood education governance structure struggles with collaboration = professional development system struggles to meet cross-sector requirements and needs birth-to-5, cross-sector state early childhood education systems. The Race to the Top–Early Learning Challenge (RTT–ELC) program encourages raising the quality of the early childhood education workforce through a unified competency framework, career pathways, and partnerships with IHEs and others. The Individuals with Disabilities Education Act (IDEA), through requirements for a comprehensive system of personnel development, provides multiple opportunities for collaboration in PD for staff working with young children who have developmental delays and disabilities. Through Title I of the Elementary and Secondary Education Act (ESEA), local schools and districts have the option of using Title I funds for preschool and school-age educators, and joint PD of educators in community-based early childhood settings and schools. Other parts of ESEA, such as Title II teacher PD and Title III supports for dual-language learners, can be a workforce resource for school and early childhood systems. Indeed, virtually every major federal funding stream has encouraged the development of cross-sector PD supports for teachers, and for some for leaders as well.

Cross-Sector Ownership

Despite the emphasis on broadened visions, the funding streams and infrastructure that support PD systems remain fragmented. To truly be integrated, PD systems must face the huge task of aligning or combining preexisting systems of preparation and support—some of which have a professionalized workforce with public support and accountability (Head Start and P–12 public education) and others that typically do not (child care). Realizing a comprehensive, integrated vision requires mechanisms for cross-sector ownership and accountability. The level of collaboration success established by the early childhood/school-age system governance often has a direct effect on the PD system, as illustrated in Figure 10.2.

In some states, PD system advisory bodies or work groups are well established and have continued effectively through governance changes to the overall early childhood/school-age system. These advisory groups can also play an inverse role to the one illustrated in Figure 10.2; they can help advance meaningful collaboration for the entire system.

No matter the age of a system or its advisory groups, an inclusive governance approach is required for integration success. Absent such an approach, sectors may be invited to the table by broad work groups, yet they may see themselves as simply contributing ideas and advising on another sector's system rather than one that benefits the entire workforce. Relying on informal coordination and collaboration produces significant barriers to

Figure 10.2. Cross-Sector Collaboration Influence from System to Subsystem

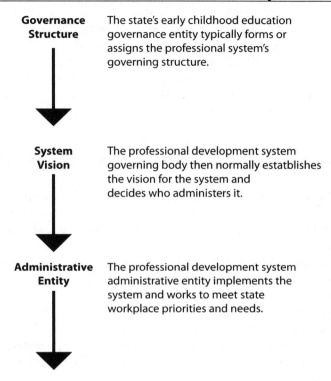

Governance Structure
The state's early childhood education governance entity typically forms or assigns the professional system's governing structure.

System Vision
The professional development system governing body then normally estatblishes the vision for the system and decides who administers it.

Administrative Entity
The professional development system administrative entity implements the system and works to meet state workplace priorities and needs.

providing PD that can meet each sector's needs and requirements, and to advancing the workforce as a whole. Formal shared governance agreements that include the commitment of cross-sector fiscal resources can increase accountability for all partners. Formalizing cross-sector accountability in governance helps ensure a system's sustainability. When governing bodies also place a premium on the continuum of PD needed for the diverse workforce—for example, by including varied levels of PD in its system vision —it also helps ensure cross-sector approval and participation.

To be effective, PD system governance must be built on trust from the early childhood/school-age workforce, the public, funders, policymakers, and other stakeholders. All of these people need to have confidence that the system leaders are authentic representatives of the field and its stakeholders, make good decisions, offer high-quality and relevant PD, know where they are taking the system and why, and can grow and sustain needed services. A clearly articulated vision for an integrated, comprehensive system provides a foundation for building this trust. If the governance structure transparently operates by and in support of the vision, it will further cement meaningful engagement and support. What type of entity the governance body designates to administer the PD system also profoundly affects the system's outreach and buy-in. The determination of the administrative entity can be one of the most important actions of the governance body. It is the administrative entity that implements the PD system and its activities; ultimately, this entity must carry out the system's vision.

GOVERNANCE AND PD SYSTEM ADMINISTRATION TYPES

For analysis and comparison purposes, we can divide PD system governance into two categories: (1) governance by state agencies, and (2) governance by community-based organizations with public/private collaborations or partnerships. The governing body typically determines how the PD system is administered and by whom. State PD systems are administered by three general types of entities: (1) state agencies, (2) IHEs, and (3) community-based organizations.

PD systems must use strategic *and* responsive approaches to meet the needs of the diverse early childhood/school-age workforce. The number of layers between the entities that administer and govern the professional system impacts its flexibility. Similarly, these layers influence the PD system's autonomy and decisionmaking authority.

Administration by State Agencies

State agencies may contract with multiple entities to carry out specific PD initiatives, while still retaining the overall system administration (see Figure 10.3). One or more stakeholder bodies may advise the state agencies and either establish or inform the mission and goals of the agency and its services. State agencies take direction from and are accountable to the governor, legislature, and federal funding.

Advantages. A major advantage of PD system administration by state agencies is that the fiscal agency is also the administrator. In this model of administration, agencies have some flexibility in the design and revision of PD programs, and their corresponding budget lines, to match the workforce's needs. Absent a contractor with additional administrative overhead, state agency–administered PD systems have more funds to spend directly on PD initiatives.

Figure 10.3. State/Territory Professional Development System Governance and Administration Entities

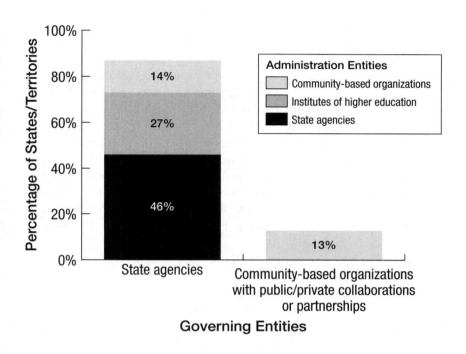

State agency–administered systems can also issue and interpret their own policies and regulations. With this authority, agencies are more easily able to align funding with policy priorities. When multiple or combined agencies share governance and administrative responsibilities for the PD system, they have the necessary authority to align policies and requirements across sectors to the benefit of the entire early childhood/school-age workforce. They may be able to relax or adapt some regulations to remove barriers and to improve coordination and collaboration across sectors. With public funds, state agencies have an established commitment to serve the public, and this commitment can help establish or reinforce public will and support for PD systems.

State agencies may also have specific budgets, resources, and sometimes departments or dedicated staff focused on outreach, research and evaluation, publication/resource development, and other services that support all of their programs and contracts.

Disadvantages. Some of the advantages of state agency administration can also be disadvantages, depending on the context. An agency's scope of work can be defined and limited by legislation or regulations. If a single state agency, such as the Department of Health and Human Services or the Department of Education, is responsible for the administration of the PD system, it can face significant challenges to being inclusive of all sectors; the system may be viewed as only targeting the primary sector that the agency serves. Agencies may also be viewed as bureaucracies that "teach to the test"—focusing on quotas for required qualifications or on certain curriculum areas that relate to current political interests, rather than on intentional and holistic career development for each member of the workforce. Early childhood/school-age professionals may also be leery of reaching out to a government office for assistance and support, especially if the PD system is in the same agency that also monitors or awards incentives to individuals or programs. Responsiveness may also challenge state agencies because of bureaucratic approval processes and policies.

Administration by Institutions of Higher Education

PD systems housed within IHEs are part of a larger program area, which takes direction from both the institution's administration and the state's board of regents/governing body. The program and the PD system may also be advised by a stakeholder group. How closely the PD system's mission aligns with that of the program area will determine if there are separate advisory bodies.

Advantages. Higher education administration can lend respected status to a PD system. A prevalent assumption is that PD offerings administered by an IHE will apply and adhere to significant quality assurance processes. IHEs typically meet national or regional accreditation criteria and have the capacity to meet standards and to maintain accountability to funders, stakeholders, and governing boards. PD offerings and system evaluation may be easier to access in these settings because IHEs typically have students and faculty engaged in ongoing research. All sectors can benefit from the advantage IHEs have in addressing articulation barriers; they can typically ensure offerings for credit or continuing education units that meet inservice requirements in any sector.

Additional example advantages of IHEs' administration include access to resources (facilities, services, and personnel), such as technology equipment and support; printing and other publication resources; libraries, current research, and related resources; financial aid services and guidance; prior learning assessments; wrap-around supports; and early childhood faculty.

Disadvantages. IHEs are usually huge systems themselves, so PD systems administered by IHEs can sometimes be "lost" in the larger institution. Further, IHEs often set and charge significant administrative costs, which can reduce the funds available for the PD system and its services.

IHEs may also be perceived as out of touch with community realities, and there may be an "intimidation factor" for some members of the early childhood/school-age workforce who have not had any formal education or who have had negative experiences with it. These professionals may not feel psychologically comfortable reaching out to PD systems that sit within IHEs.

Administration by Community-Based Organizations

Early childhood/school-age, community-based organizations include childcare resource and referral agencies, professional/membership associations, advocacy or action alliances, and others. These organizations typically have broad-based stakeholder advisory or governing bodies. These bodies are responsible for setting organizational policies and priorities, which may include PD system advising.

Advantages. Perhaps the greatest advantage of community-based PD system administration is the location of the organization. Because they are in communities, these organizations are closer to the community and can be more attuned with community needs. Their staff and leadership often reflect the diversity of the community and the early childhood/school-age field; many have worked in direct service in the field and serve as role models for vertical career progression. Often, early childhood/school-age issues are the sole or primary focus of community-based organizations that administer state PD systems. This singular focus helps these organizations dedicate staff with relevant experience to leadership roles in the system administration. Community organizations can also advocate for the workforce and its individual and collective needs—something that state agencies clearly cannot do and that IHEs may limit.

Community-based organizations can be more nimble than IHEs or state agencies in rolling out services or in developing and sharing resources, as they often don't have the same layers of required approvals. This reduced policy vetting can also allow community-based organizations to be perceived as more transparent with communication. They often have more flexibility to experiment with and use technology for outreach and delivery. They can more quickly adapt to and adopt technologically savvy methods of outreach and engagement that target the younger and next generation of the early childhood/school-age field.

Disadvantages. A significant challenge for community-based PD system administration is quality assurance, which is exacerbated by decentralization. In some cases, the community-based organizations do not have the capacity (human and technical) to provide accountability and reporting for the whole system to stakeholders and policymakers. Decentralization can also limit or complicate opportunities to advance comprehensive, statewide articulation.

Community-based organizations can also be challenged by a lack of resources. They are typically small organizations that do not have access to the resource development, printing, research, and other facility perks and staff expertise that larger IHEs and state agencies have.

CONCLUSIONS

Broad PD visions place value on integrated systems. If the vision for a state PD system is to support and sustain an effective cross-sector workforce, then the system governance and administration must consider the workforce as a whole. The integrated PD system also needs to make sure it attends to individual needs. The potential benefits of integrated PD systems begin with a cross-sector vision and are nurtured by governance that promotes innovative approaches to the professionalization of the entire workforce.

No matter where the PD system sits within the early childhood education system, what entity governs it, or how it is administered, there are advantages to leverage and challenges to face. A PD system that has authentic cross-sector governance and buy-in can build an integrated vision. The administrative entity must then help early childhood and school-age professionals get to this vision together. And they all must recognize, respect, and build the system to be responsive to the fact that individuals, sectors, and their preexisting systems are not starting from the same place. Diverse options are needed to improve practice, and to support and retain an excellent workforce.

The key to success in any governance design is to ensure that representatives of *all* the early childhood/school-age sectors are actively and equitably engaged in the visioning, system-building, integration, and implementation work. Only with an inclusive, cross-sector vision and approach to both governance and administration will states achieve high-quality services for all young children and their families.

RESOURCES FOR FURTHER READING: INTEGRATED PD SYSTEMS

- LeMoine, S. (2008). *Workforce Designs: A Policy Blueprint for State Early Childhood PD Systems*. Washington, DC: NAEYC. Retrieved from www.naeyc.org/files/naeyc/file/policy/ecwsi/ Workforce_Designs.pdf
- National Center on Child Care PD Systems and Workforce Initiatives (PDW Center). (2014). Strengthening the Early Childhood and School-Age Workforce: A Tool to Improve Workplace Conditions, Compensation, and Access to PD. Washington, DC: PDW Center, jointly funded by ACF's Office of Child Care and Office of Head Start, ZERO TO THREE. Retrieved from https://childcareta.acf.hhs.gov//resource/strengthening-early-childhood-and-school-age-workforce

CHAPTER 11

Family and Community Engagement in Early Childhood Education Governance

Thomas Rendon

Somewhat paradoxically, engaging families and communities in early childhood systems governance is both risky and essential. Involving them is risky because family and community involvement can be disruptive to the planning, decisionmaking, and administrative functions of governance. Yet, involving them is essential because their role is of paramount importance in the lives of young children. So, how can families and communities be engaged with early childhood governance, avoiding the risks while leveraging the deepest potential?

This chapter gives a simple, direct answer: by making sure that engagement is deep and mutual, that a wide range of opportunities for engagement is available, and that the manner of engagement provides true power-sharing. The way early childhood governance does this is by creating or transforming its structures and the way it does its business (planning, oversight, coordination, and accountability). Given the abundant attention to creating effective governance, this chapter considers how the structures of early childhood governance and the practices of governing entities should be changed to engage families and communities, not only in the work of governance itself but in the broader enterprise of building early childhood systems.

I begin by discussing engagement in the hopes of recovering its true meaning, since its overuse has weakened our understanding of the term. Then I discuss what the structures and activities of early childhood governance should look like to better accomplish effective engagement. As part of this second discussion, I suggest a set of practices that I call "norms of engagement," which may inspire new thinking about how we can best engage families and communities.

WHAT IS ENGAGEMENT?

I define *engagement* as intentional and influential involvement. Its etymological roots are found in the Middle French term meaning "to be placed under an oath," as a couple becomes "engaged" when they commit to each other to be married. Its origins are more akin to the older word *betrothed* (which also means to be under a "truth" or "troth") rather than to its common usage as a synonym for *connection* or *involvement*. The connotative link to matrimonial commitment reminds us that engagement is a binding commitment and relationship-based. In other words, it is about partnership and mutuality, not provider-client or representative-constituent relations.

Unpacking further the definition above, *intention* is allied to the idea of commitment and insists that involvement is done with clear purpose, accompanied by goals, plans, and measures. The idea of *influence* means that involvement is consequential. If family or community engagement has any value to governance, it is because family and community members have direct influence on early childhood programs and services.

BUILDING GOVERNANCE STRUCTURES THAT ENGAGE FAMILIES AND COMMUNITIES

Early childhood education (ECE) systems, at their best, are an integrated collection of programs and services that serve young children and their families, and governance of these systems is composed of "the structures, processes, and policies that enable a system to function consistently, effectively, and efficiently" (Kauerz & Kagan, 2012, p. 88). Governance fulfills its responsibilities first by creating an organizational structure with defined roles for each unit within the structure. A lot of literature about early childhood governance has focused on the types of governance structures states have adopted and which ones are best suited to driving positive and substantive change or most effective at overall systems coordination (Bruner, Stover-Wright, Gebhard, & Hibbard, 2004; Dichter, 2012; Kagan & Kauerz, 2008; Kauerz & Kagan, 2012; Ponder, 2012; Regenstein & Lipper, 2013). The relevant question here is how accessible governance structures are to families and communities.

Structures That Expand Engagement

Engagement of families and communities in governance typically means service on boards and committees operating under the auspices of a particular governance entity where important decisions are made. But the specific structures of governance should not themselves become barriers for engagement by families or communities. If board or committee service means attendance at monthly meetings scheduled during working hours, most family members are immediately excluded. So, instead of having only one means of involvement, multiple opportunities for engagement should be offered to ensure active engagement by as many family and community members as possible.

Besides direct board or committee service, service on ad hoc advisory boards or focus groups is another way to involve family and community members. Because it can be assumed that family and community members are extremely busy, providing opportunities to participate in work teams using telephone or Internet-based meetings, synchronous or asynchronous gatherings through email, or web-based interfaces using smartphones or electronic tablets should be considered. Electronic surveys are simple ways to take the pulse of many people quickly, without placing a heavy burden on the time. Sometimes technological solutions are out of reach for families of low income, but access to texting through cellphones and more advanced communication, especially with smartphones, is increasingly common (Pew, 2014; Smith, 2012). Any solution needs to be amenable to the families or community members targeted for engagement.

Informal groups, such as advisory councils, are often undervalued because they appear to have no authority or decisionmaking power. On the contrary, they wield very specific power: to influence. Although they are not the final arbiter when it comes to making something happen, they set the agenda and promote specific action that powerful governing bodies cannot/ should not overlook. The surest way to get more involvement in advisory groups is to take their input seriously and to put it into effect.

When structures are opened up and allow for multiple means of engagement, the opinions and perspectives of family and community members can enrich the conversation, and the resulting solutions are likely to find broader agreement by the public.

Structures That Effectively Address Power Issues

Early childhood governance is about organizing authority and oversight of the ECE system. Its effectiveness is determined by its power to implement decisions, to shape the nature and accountability of early childhood programs and services. Not surprisingly, governing entities recruit people of influence and power to improve their ability to make change. Family and community representatives are not necessarily people of influence; their skills or political influence may not be sufficient to make them effective change-makers at a local or state level where governing bodies wield influence. Ferguson and Stoutland (1999) observed that the more connected a community organization is to its community members, the less likely it is to be connected to sources of economic and political power.

The same is true for ECE systems. The more connected governance structures are to state authority, by having, for instance, policy oversight over substantial state and federal revenue streams (e.g., Individual with Disabilities in Education, Child Care Development Fund, state-funded preschool), the less likely those systems are to have real, day-to-day connection with children and families. Ferguson and Stoutland's insight helps explain why governance structures, especially as they are seeking to expand their influence and impact, are reluctant to engage families and communities and more likely to engage individuals who are perceived as power and influence brokers. Given this inclination in organizational behavior, governance processes must be set up to ensure broad community and family participation despite the relative powerlessness of some or many community members.

This is not to say that families and communities are without power. They are, in fact, very powerful, wielding enormous influence over the developmental trajectory of children, precisely an area where early childhood governance might want to exert some influence as well. This common goal of raising healthy and successful children would recommend alliances. In fact, the structures of governance and the avenues of participation organized to leverage family and community power are often missing. Instead, the inherent influence that families and communities have over the well-being of children is ignored and trivialized. Or worse, their influence is wrested away from them and placed in the hands of professional caregivers, teachers, social workers, and home visitors. Consider how often early childhood services such as health care, child care and preschool, and family support are performed in a way that service providers, acting as the expert and professional, usurp the traditional roles of family members as caregivers, educators, or even responsible parents. Of course, there are times when such action is necessary, such as in cases of child abuse or neglect. But even in these situations, such action, however justifiable, means the disempowerment of families and therefore is a step away from engagement.

By recognizing the power of families and communities in raising children, early childhood systems governance should view families and communities as essential partners. Power-sharing with families and communities keeps families engaged and generates lasting, significant outcomes for children in terms of better early social emotional health, health outcomes, improved school readiness, and later academic success (Cook, Roggman, & Boyce,

2012; Fabricius, Sokol, Diaz, & Braver, 2012; Fan & Chen, 2001; Ferguson, Ramos, Rudo, & Wood, 2008; Niemeier, Hektner, & Enger, 2012).

BUILDING GOVERNANCE ACTIVITIES
THAT ENGAGE FAMILIES AND COMMUNITIES

In considering the engagement of families and communities in governance activities, I suggest two broad roles for governance entities: (1) to support families and communities in fulfilling their roles in helping children grow up healthy and successful; and (2) to ensure that families and communities have a voice in the planning, oversight, coordination, and accountability of the system. The first function is about making governance activities work in partnership with families and communities around the shared task of raising healthy and successful children. Regarding the second, Charles Bruner and his colleagues remind us that "governance requires consent of the governed to endure" (Bruner, Stover-Wright, Gebhard, & Hibbard, 2004, p. 10). It is a sentiment as much about the moral authority of governance as it is about the making of good governance.

Supporting the Roles of Families

The Parent, Family, and Community Engagement Framework from Head Start lists seven goals (Office of Head Start, 2011). I collapse these seven into three broader roles of families: as caregivers, educators, and advocates. The activities of governing entities (planning, oversight, coordination, and accountability) should promote and support these roles. To support the caregiver role, governance activities should address family well-being and positive parent-child relationships. When governing bodies plan, they should assess the status of family well-being and parent-child relationships and determine appropriate responses to positively impact these areas, set goals that address family safety and financial self-sufficiency so families can provide for children's basic needs, design and fund services that teach parents skills so they can have nurturing and responsive relationships with their children, and develop monitoring systems to ensure that these services actually work. For coordination, it means convening organizations whose work affects family well-being and making sure they have a common vision, are communicating with one another, and are collaborating when possible.

Head Start provides a useful example. Federal regulations require grantees to assess the needs of the community prior as part of receiving a grant, so the services are addressing local issues surrounding family well-being. They also call for each enrolled family to draft a family development plan where the needs of the family can become part of the services and referrals provided as part of the comprehensive services offered. The lesson here for ECE governance is to embed these desired behaviors into policy and regulation.

One can imagine a similar approach to support a family's educator or advocate role. For example, governing bodies can establish policies and promote practices that ensure families have the skills to support their children's learning, encourage family members to pursue their own educational dreams, or help families develop networks of peers and connect to the wider community so they are better able to fulfill an advocate role. The point here is not that governing entities are responsible for directly supporting families in all these ways; *rather, they are responsible for making sure, as part of their planning and oversight functions, some entity is engaging in such practices.* Governing entities should use their power to ensure practices that promote the roles of families are established, implemented, and evaluated. In Iowa, the Early Childhood Iowa Stakeholder Alliance convened a work group to develop family support standards. At first, the standards were voluntary, and then they became the basis for a program certification process. Finally, they became a requirement for recipients of state funding. The Alliance established and implemented the standards to the extent of its statutory power. But then the state legislature used its authority to make the standards required. The focus was on best practices, and the mechanism for accomplishing it was through the strategic use of governance.

Supporting the Roles of Communities

The role of communities is to maintain supportive environments so that needed services are available to its residents. When one thinks of all the essential services children and families need (health, mental health, nutrition, early learning, family support, child welfare, and special needs/early intervention), all are delivered within a community context. The community capacity to amass adequate resources and capital determines the degree to which services are available and their quality. Therefore, governance activities should coordinate with communities to ensure equitable access to resources. Governing bodies can model broad planning efforts to show how multiple community sectors (governmental, business, and philanthropic) can be engaged to identify and use all available capital (physical, human, social, and economic).

While Cedar Valley Promise (CVP), a county-based citizen-led board that does collaboration and systems development in the community, determines funding for projects, the final decision lies with its board, which by policy excludes representatives from agencies who are potential recipients of funding. But to ensure equitable distribution of resources, an advisory group made up of these agency representatives works together to make recommendations to the board based on a shared commitment to the organizations that most need funding and that address the priorities of Cedar Valley Promise. Between the CVP board and the advisory board, broad and transparent planning efforts engage government, business, community agencies, foundations, and parents (K. Young-Kent, personal communication, August 14, 2014).

Ensuring Families and Communities a Voice

The second role of ECE governance entities in relation to family and community is to ensure that they have a voice in governance decisionmaking. The comprehensive and integrated nature of consolidated governance allows for "norms of engagement" to be woven into ECE systems. These norms are a collection of practices that early childhood governance can promote through policy and regulations, and through the programs and services it oversees or coordinates. Based on the definition for engagement provided earlier in this chapter, three categories of norms are considered: norms of involvement, influence, and intentionality.

Norms of Involvement. Governance structures that involve families and communities include clear visions about how to promote involvement within its own internal structure as well as within the programs, services, and systems it oversees. Norms of involvement include:

- Providing multiple opportunities for involvement along a continuum from passive to active (this means different kinds of involvement in different kinds of activities, including determining issues, problem solving, planning, decisionmaking, and resource allocation, along with numerous explicit invitations to join a group or attend a meeting)
- Valuing all involvement as "sweat equity" to reinforce the belief that everyone who benefits from a service should be expected to contribute to it
- Recruiting professional staff at the system or program level from the ranks of families and communities

When early childhood systems engage in evaluation and needs assessment, the reports and their results should include information about programs and services that are relevant to families and community members and this information should be made readily available to them. In the case of evaluation based on child outcome data, deliberate strategies to explain the assessment process and its results should be common practice (Bruner, Agnamba, Calderon, & Simons, 2013). Furthermore, the measures of quality used to assess programs should include how well they engage families and communities. For example, family and community engagement could be part of states' Quality Rating and Improvement Systems (QRIS).

Norms of Influence. Governance structures that involve families and communities should establish norms of influence: consistent ways in which family and community members can influence the workings of governance. Governing entities must be open to outside influence, especially if family and community members are not actually at the table. Even activities with a less direct effect on families and communities, such as the design and accountability of services or the reporting of broad-measure outcomes, should show transparency and educate outsiders on how the system actually operates. Norms of influence include:

- Ensuring input on key decisions
- Employing social, public, and community-based media to keep the general public and targeted groups well informed
- Using direct action strategies when expressing opinion is not sufficient to make desired change; such strategies might include nonviolent resistance such as sit-ins, occupation of public space, or the disruption of meetings

Norms of Intentionality. The norms of intentionality are necessary to make sure that involvement and influence are realized. Intentionality does not depend on chance or good fortune but is realized through planned action. Norms of intentionality include:

- Goal-setting
- Strategic planning
- Successful implementation

This norm embraces what implementation science has shown to be a more purposeful, active, and effective approach to implementation (Fixsen & Blasé, 2009). Family and community engagement deserves the same seriousness and deliberateness as any endeavor embarked upon for the sake of children.

CONCLUSIONS

This chapter began by noting that the engagement of families and communities is both essential and risky. To mitigate the risk, early childhood systems governance tends to make engagement superficial so the outside influence of family or community members is less disruptive. Such practice ignores the fact that governance needs the engagement of families and communities to be powerful, effective, and legitimate. The mechanisms of early childhood governance can begin to address the essential but risky dilemma by promoting a consistent ethos that services are always delivered *with* families and communities and not *to* families and communities.

Early childhood governance can build flexible and dynamic structures that allow for wide-ranging participation in many different forms. Governance practice can make it a matter of habit to seize power and give it back to families and communities so it becomes their prerogative to determine how resources are best used, how power is best exercised, and who should control which decisions. That is what real engagement is about: returning power and control to families and communities.

It is hard for early childhood professionals to hear this because, as a field, early childhood has been consistently marginalized, the needs of young children and their families have not been taken seriously, and their rightful share of public resources has been plainly shorted. The successes that have been achieved have been hard-won, and although the importance of early childhood has gained prominence as never before, no one is arguing that that the struggle is over. In fact, before it's over, I invite the reader here to consider how marginalization is an opportunity to do governance "right": governance not for the consolidation of power, but for its democratization. Because early childhood only involves a very small share of political or economic power in this country, sharing what little is available may be the way to arrive at governance that represents the best impulses for public good.

REFERENCES

Bruner, C., Agnamba, L. A., Calderon, M., & Simons, K. A. (2013). *Families know best*. Boston, MA: The BUILD Initiative.

Bruner, C., Stover-Wright, M., Gebhard, B., & Hibbard, S. (2004). *Building an early learning system: The ABCs of planning and governance structures*. Des Moines, IA: State Early Childhood Policy Technical Assistance Network (SECPTAN) and BUILD Initiative. Retrieved from www.finebynine.org/uploaded/file/SECPTAN_Build_PROOF.pdf

Cook, G., Roggman, L., & Boyce, L. (2012). Fathers' and mothers' cognitive stimulation in early play with toddlers: Predictors of 5th grade reading and math. *Family Science, 2*, 131–145.

Dichter, H. (2012). Governance in early childhood systems: The view from Pennsylvania. In K. Kauerz & S. L. Kagan (Eds.), *Early childhood systems: Transforming early learning* (pp. 245–251). New York, NY: Teachers College Press.

Fabricius, W. V., Sokol, K. R., Diaz, P., & Braver, S. L. (2012). Parenting time, parent conflict, parent-child relationships, and children's physical health. In K. Kuehnle & L. Drozd (Eds.), *Parent plan evaluations: Applied research for the family court* (pp. 188–213). New York, NY: Oxford University Press.

Fan, X., & Chen, M. (2001). Parental involvement and students' academic achievement: A meta-analysis. *Educational Psychology Review, 13*(1), 1–22.

Ferguson, C., Ramos, M., Rudo, Z., & Wood, L. (2008). *The school family connection: Looking at the larger picture. A review of current literature.* Austin, TX: National Center for Family and Community Connections with Schools (SEDL).

Ferguson, R. F., & Stoutland, S. E. (1999). Reconceiving the community development field. In R. F. Ferguson & W. T. Dickens (Eds.), *Urban problems and community development* (pp. 33–75). Washington, DC: Brookings Institute.

Fixsen, D. L., & Blasé, K. A. (2009, January). *Implementation: The missing link between research and practice. NIRN Implementation Brief #1.* Chapel Hill, NC: The University of North Carolina, FPG, NIRN. Retrieved from http://miblsi. cenmi.org/LinkClick.aspx?fileticket=T6mQAnz5pak%3D&tabid=1194

Kagan, S. L., & Kauerz, K. (2008). Governing American early care and education: Shifting from government to governance and from form to function. In S. Feeney, A. Galper, & C. Seefeldt (Eds.), *Continuing issues in early childhood education* (3rd ed., pp. 12–32). Columbus, OH: Pearson Merrill Prentice Hall.

Kauerz, K., & Kagan, S. L. (2012). Governance and early childhood systems. In K. Kauerz & S. L. Kagan (Eds.), *Early childhood systems: Transforming early learning* (pp. 87–103). New York, NY: Teachers College Press.

Niemeier, B. S., Hektner, J. M., & Enger, K. B. (2012). Parent participation in weight-related health interventions for children and adolescents: A systematic review and meta-analysis. *Preventive medicine, 55*(1), 3–13.

Office of Head Start. (2011). *The Head Start parent, family, and community engagement framework: Promoting family engagement and school readiness, from prenatal to age 8.* Washington, DC: Author. Retrieved from http://eclkc.ohs.acf. hhs.gov/hslc/standards/IMs/2011/pfce-framework.pdf

Pew Charitable Trusts. (2014). *Pew internet and American life project.* Retrieved from pewinternet.org.

Ponder, K. (2012). A state vision for an early childhood system: Meaningful governance. In K. Kauerz & S. L. Kagan (Eds.), *Early childhood systems: Transforming early learning* (pp. 41–46). New York, NY: Teachers College Press.

Regenstein, E., & Lipper, K. (2013). *A framework for choosing a state-level early childhood governance system.* Boston, MA: BUILD Initiative. Retrieved from www. buildinitiative.org/Portals/0/Uploads/Documents/Early%20Childhood%20 Governance%20for%20Web.pdf

Smith, A. (2012, March). *Nearly half of American adults are smartphone owners.* Retrieved from http://pewinternet.org/Reports/2012/Smartphone-Update-2012/ Findings.aspx

THE FUTURE OF EARLY CHILDHOOD GOVERNANCE

CHAPTER 12

Looking Ahead

Governance and the Role of Leadership

Susan Hibbard

Despite being long-ignored and deeply underfunded, the early childhood education field is making advances at dizzying speed. Its relative newness is evidenced, in part, by the abundance of frameworks that characterize the field. Many early childhood efforts continue to be propelled by the first goal of the National Education Goals Panel established in 1989, which posited the objective that all children in the United States will start school ready to learn (Shepard, Kagan, & Wurtz, 1998). Other efforts are framed as strides toward attempts to address disparities among children and to produce equitable outcomes. Since 2011, foundation leaders and others in the early childhood field have popularized the goal of all children being able to read proficiently by 3rd grade. Still others describe their objective as ensuring that the first 1,000 days of a child's life provide a strong foundation for healthy development and learning, because these are the most significant days, generally speaking, in determining a child's trajectory.

Regardless of the framing, these strategic approaches are all aspects of systems-building efforts—an early learning system, early care and education system, or early childhood system. The early childhood field lacks a shared lexicon, which parallels the divergence in describing the goal of supporting children's learning and development. These system visions differ in their age focus: for example, birth or prenatal to age 5 or 8. They also vary in whether education is the focal point (sometimes singling out literacy) or one of several. An early childhood system is frequently envisioned as a system of systems—matching the basic needs of the child with child-serving systems: family support to strengthen families and ensure secure, nurturing relationships; health and mental health to ensure physical and social–emotional well-being; and early learning and development to provide children with safe, enriching environments and experiences with adults who foster learning and development.

This chapter initiates a discussion of the relationships between governance, systemic advances in early childhood, and systems-building leadership. As will be illustrated, vision and leadership are necessary components for any governance system to thrive and have lasting impact.

In 2006, the Early Childhood Systems Working Group depicted the core elements of the system (Figure 12.1), including three systemic visions that, together, create thriving children and communities: early learning experiences, family support and engagement, and health and mental health.

Implementing any of these systemic visions requires governance, as the programs, services, and policies related to young children have traditionally been fragmented, siloed, and rooted in categorical funding streams that persist as barriers to families and young children gaining access to what should be a seamless (user-friendly) continuum of services and programs designed to meet their multifaceted developmental needs. The unprecedented focus on young children and on early learning in this country during the past decade, however, has also led to accelerated creation and innovation in early childhood systems building and its governance. Regenstein (Chapter 3) provides a general classification of the most common current governance approaches among states. But changing the locus of specific programs, or reorganizing, does not alone alter their functions or automatically promote effectiveness. An effective model of governance should create coherence among policies and services, reduce fragmentation and uneven quality, and be a standard-bearer for equity in early childhood. This requires vision and leadership.

This chapter acknowledges the importance of all kinds of leaders in the early childhood field. My focus, however, is on leadership for systems-building in early learning and, more broadly, in early childhood. In addressing this topic, I seek to discuss who these leaders are or can be, what additional kinds of leaders they need to nurture and support, and what attributes assist them in their efforts.

QUESTIONS FOR A YOUNG FIELD

Early childhood systems development is young; the early childhood systems are even younger. This means that leaders are working in ill-defined arenas that are still taking shape, and are doing so with less-than-adequate information to guide the work. Some areas of work have an extensive research base; others do not. There is much that we still do not fully understand, and those areas in which the field has gained the most ground are often the ones that have also generated the most urgent questions.

Figure 12.1. A Fully Coordinated Early Learning System

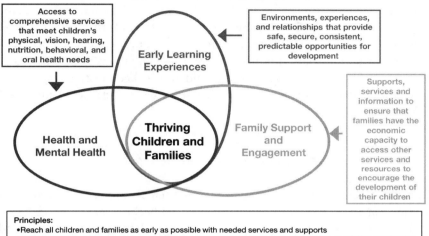

What Should a Fully Coordinated State Early Childhood Development and Learning System Deliver?

Access to comprehensive services that meet children's physical, vision, hearing, nutrition, behavioral, and oral health needs

Environments, experiences, and relationships that provide safe, secure, consistent, predictable opportunities for development

Early Learning Experiences

Supports, services and information to ensure that families have the economic capacity to access other services and resources to encourage the development of their children

Health and Mental Health

Thriving Children and Families

Family Support and Engagement

Principles:
- Reach all children and families as early as possible with needed services and supports
- Reflect and respect the strengths, needs, values, languages, cultures, and communities of children and families
- Genuinely include and effectively accommodate children with special needs
- Ensure stability and continuity of services along a continuum from prenatal to school entry
- Ease access for families and transitions for children
- Catalyze investment and foster innovation   2-25-11

We know rating the quality of care does not alone improve service quality. But, do we know the most effective strategies that do improve quality? Have we even defined quality in ways that are conducive to creating successful early learning opportunities for all young children? How can we more fully understand the role of the demographics of families, children, and communities, and then use that information effectively? How can we hold programs accountable in ways that truly result in quality improvement and that address disparities? And, how can we support families and communities to meet the needs of children, whether they are in formal care or not? How can we build bridges and advance communication among all the people, services, programs, and systems that are part of the fabric of the child and family's life so that the whole child is supported to grow and develop, while retaining eagerness and readiness to learn and thrive?

Some of the pressing questions focus on governance: Does consolidated governance promote efficiencies? Does housing early childhood in education have more pros than cons? How does it impact the connection with health and mental health? And, even more fundamentally, are we on the right track? Are our federal and state initiatives using the right drivers for systems change? These questions, and many more, cause anxiety and disturbance.

In this period of the field's youth, a little restlessness and impatience is a good thing. Historian Laurel Thatcher Ulrich is quoted as saying, "Well-behaved women seldom make history." The same might be said for the individuals working in the early childhood arena. Public-sector "leaders" often follow an unspoken rule not to rock the boat. Change, however, is at the core of development. Systems development requires taking risks, running trials, and making errors—using the very best data and evidence available, but having the confidence to keep testing, trying, innovating, and always being open to new information and better ideas—in other words, leading.

LEADERSHIP APPROACHES IN ECE

In the early childhood field, leadership has been examined from many different stances. Goffin and Washington (2007) beckon early care and education leaders to speak for themselves, without letting policymakers and advocates define the challenges and solutions for the field. Others have recognized the critical role that school superintendents and principals play in embracing all young children (from birth), stressing the need for alignment of K–12 and early learning (Ochshorn, 2000; Ponder, 2011). This stance often stresses the need for innovations and practices in early childhood to be "pushed up" into the school space (NAEYC, 2012). Still others (Stoney, 2013; Stoney & Blank, 2011) have underscored the need to build new shared leadership in the market-based early care and education sector, where leadership is often centered on a single program director, who must play myriad leadership roles with little or no support. Some have looked cross-system (Bruner, 2013a) and have reminded us of the enormous potential of a medical home and primary care physicians who regularly see many more children in the first years of those children's lives than do child-care centers. Therefore, physicians are plausible players in the identification of maternal depression, family stress, and developmental delays in a child. And, Fullan (2002) has focused us on the need for leadership and peer support as part of a culture of change.

NEW IDEAS ABOUT LEADERSHIP FOR SYSTEMS-BUILDING

In his first national evaluation essay for the BUILD Initiative, discussed in more detail later in the chapter, Dr. Charles Bruner, executive director of the Child and Family Policy Center, cited Harold Williams's advice to funders of innovation: Invest in people rather than in work plans (Bruner, 2003). Bruner went on to describe the initiative's approach as one aligned with Margaret Mead's famous quote: "Never doubt that a few committed people can change the world; indeed, that is the only thing that ever has" (cited in Bruner, 2003, p. 12). BUILD selected states not based on gubernatorial leadership or governance structures but on the presence of a critical mass of identified and well-positioned committed individuals whom the initiative could support with resources to move forward an agenda. Supporting the potential of creative and passionate leaders, wherever they sit, remains central to systems-building work today. Leadership is critical on multiple levels: at the executive, mid-level, and local and community levels. Leaders must also be invested in and engage together in a multitiered network.

Executive and Mid-Level Leadership

Top-level leadership is most easily recognized. And little equals the authority of a governor with a bold early childhood vision, such as North Carolina's Jim Hunt or, more recently, Pennsylvania's Ed Rendell. Identifying, cultivating, and nurturing such leaders is often the work of advocacy groups. One of the key results of a governor's leadership is the ability to set a big vision and to have the power to direct agencies to achieve it. But these top leaders are transient, their administrations' time is limited, and it is always many leaders working together that are needed to build successful systems.

After summarizing several state-level case studies focused on leadership development in early childhood systems efforts, Coffman and Wright (2011) suggested that although top-level leadership is often central to momentous, rapid progress, most of the time, systems-building efforts are slow and comprise gradual changes. Some efforts are not even about forward motion but instead are defensive actions to thwart regressive changes. Coffman and Wright emphasized the critical need for leadership, other than at the top, during these slower times.

Leaders at other levels must implement the big leaps forward or keep pushing the agenda when the political and economic environments are less conducive to major change. States that ignore leadership development in the middle tiers—for example, administrators, agency workers, and frontline staff—will be frustrated by a lack of progress during what many in systems-building perceive as "down times" (Coffman & Wright, 2011, p. 6).

Recognition of the rapid changes that can be secured when early childhood supporters are in positions of power with control over human and fiscal resources directs systems-building leaders to seek out and support top-level leaders. The short-lived nature of that power, conversely, persuades systems-building leaders to focus also on continuously fostering a climate in which even less-than-supportive leaders will view early childhood issues as salient.

These systems leaders must also identify and implement strategies to institutionalize the advances being made so they will be sustained despite political leadership transitions. This focus on formalizing and embedding the advances made is tempered by the need to maintain openness to new ideas and further advances. This tension between securing and sustaining achievements and maintaining commitment to the ongoing process of development is ushering in a continuous improvement perspective that early childhood systems leaders are just beginning to delineate.

Local and Community Leadership

Even in times of rapid, state-led change, systems-building is not likely to succeed without leadership and ownership at the local or community level, as well as among many stakeholders, including service providers themselves. Not all decisions can be made effectively at the state level (or by state bureaucrats). State leaders need to examine how much planning and decisionmaking should "devolve" to the community level. In doing so, state leaders also need to determine what parameters, training, support, and oversight is necessary at the state level to ensure that the discretion provided at the community level is exercised effectively (Bruner, Wright, Gebhard, & Hibbard, 2004).

Both state and local leaders are essential to effective planning, implementation, and revision of early childhood systems efforts, as is two-way communication between these leaders at different levels. State-level efforts need to be informed by local leadership. Similarly, state and local leaders need to think critically about what systems are needed at the provider level to ensure that policy is effectively applied and dollars are well spent. Local leaders are key to creating feedback loops that can empower providers and families who remain underserved and communities that are underresourced to help design strategies to close the achievement gap. Local-level efforts require the support, infrastructure, and resources of the state, and often of the private sector as well.

Investing in Leaders

The nature of early childhood leadership has changed over time as the field has gained experience in the support role and as the context has shifted. Previously, support largely consisted of funding and instruction or direction;

now, it is more broadly understood to include the development of learning communities, communities of practice, and other vehicles for mutual support and peer exchange. Where once information exchange was largely unidirectional (researchers or philanthropists explained or funded best practices or prioritized strategies), now leaders who have guided the design, implementation, or revision of some aspect(s) of early childhood systems are recognized as experts with critical knowledge and experience to share in the service of achieving better outcomes for children.

Leaders of early childhood systems, or of systems development efforts, are often isolated within their structure and within their state. The impatience to do better for children and families can mean taking on unpopular issues or holding positions that are not widely accepted. Even when not isolated or ostracized, the leader's role can be a delicate balance. He or she may hold the vision, but lack some of the contacts, knowledge, and skills needed to advance the work. Supporting systems leaders requires networks, too. A network of peers can share successes and failures, contacts, and resources. A network of peers can sustain the momentum and replenish the energy needed.

Leadership as a Multitiered Network

States might benefit from thinking about leadership development and the activation of leaders in terms of network development (Coffman & Wright, 2011). Not only can systems leaders be positioned in any number of structures and play a myriad of different roles but the effective systems leader has a perspective and worldview that highly values the role of partnership and collaboration and the imperative of understanding, embracing, and engaging multiple other leaders from various perspectives, positions, and sectors.

The image of a network with multiple, connected hubs and subnetworks represents the vision of a system of systems with leaders exerting influence, creating impact, and leading at multiple levels. Some hubs may become more visible or more relevant to advances in some time frames, while others may be in a different context. As indicated earlier, leaders of early childhood systems can be placed in government—at the top, leading an agency, or mid-level. Leaders can be in nonprofit advocacy organizations or in quasi-governmental groups. The job title or locus is not the driver; the strength and clarity of the vision is. The leader envisions an ever-growing network that shares information and connects services and people to support the whole child and his or her family, with its culture, language, and community.

SYSTEMS LEADERSHIP CASE STUDY

State leadership is one part of a multifaceted approach to systems-building within states, local governments, and communities, and among service providers. In state after state, year after year, the need to develop and support leadership at each of these levels has been underscored. In 2002, the Early Childhood Funders Collaborative designed and launched the BUILD Initiative as an alternative, systemic approach to improving outcomes for our youngest children (Early Childhood Funders Collaborative, Mission Statement, January 2002). Here, I look at the initiative and a case study in Ohio.

The BUILD Initiative

From the outset, core leaders of the initiative (from philanthropy, state advocacy organizations, state agencies, and research and evaluation organizations) described the initiative as helping states take their next best steps. In 2004, BUILD produced its theory of change, which indicated the critical role not just of political leaders in states, but also of agency and mid-level leadership (Bruner, Gebhard, & Hibbard, 2004). Inherent in the theory, or at least simultaneous to its development, was a strong undercurrent that big leaps forward could only take place with executive (and at least some legislative) leadership. Yet, there was a lack of clarity regarding systems-building efforts—how they were to be sustained and led (and who could do that leading) when gubernatorial leadership was weak, or worse yet, damaging to early childhood progress.

Effective systems-building requires strategic thinking and systems' leadership. Systems' leadership is not necessarily exerted by those who manage the coordination among agencies or who direct consolidated or newly created offices. Systems leaders are those who recognize the ongoing, complex, and interconnected nature of systems-building. They may crave a linear progression, but its absence is not seen as an insurmountable barrier. They recognize that even small decisions about policies and practices can impact the overall system. They seek the next right steps to make advances. The steps aren't chosen because they fall in a leader's purview, but because systems leaders press forward toward desired results and/or aid in the achievement of interim outcomes. They think and act systemically in the real world, where needs and opportunities are in dynamic tension.

Successful systems-building efforts have shown (Bruner, 2013b):

1. *Leadership occurs at many levels.* Several types of leadership are
   essential for early childhood systems-building: political, state, and
   local policy; state administrative; practice (e.g., program directors);
   and grassroots and grasstops.
2. *Policy matters, but it is not absolute.* The ways that, and the locus
   from which, leadership is exercised are critical to advances, and
   they change over time; such alterations are related to but not solely
   contingent upon the political climate.
3. *Leadership can, and will, change.* No one type of leader will lead
   systems-building over time; different leverage points will be more
   or less important at different levels. Bruner and colleagues (2004)
   offered a construction analogy to make this point: "Building is done
   in stages. These stages often require different workers with various
   skills, talents, and resources. Architects are needed at one stage of
   building a house or school, while plumbers and painters are needed
   at another stage" (p. 9). They also noted the limits of the analogy,
   however, because in systems-building multiple activities are often
   simultaneous and not sequential.

Building Leadership in Ohio: A Case Study

The structures supporting systems-building work, the key players, and
changes in leadership over time are all documented in a Community
Research Partners case study of Ohio's systems-building work from 2003 to
2008 (Beckwith, 2009). An outside perspective of Ohio's early childhood efforts during those years would likely have been that the work BUILD funded and supported was positive and well worth the investment, but likely
unrelated to advancing systemic change. The case study, however, proffered
the perspective that Ohio's BUILD leaders had strategically selected areas of
focus, structure, and systems leadership based on the logical and the possible, given the prevailing political realities.

When the BUILD Initiative began its work with Ohio in 2002, executive state-level leadership for early childhood was lacking. However, state
agency administrators, mid-level leaders, local policy and practice leaders,
and advocates of many kinds shared the vision of building a system of supports and services for young children.

The initiative did not require a particular structure for or pathway to
early childhood systems work. Thus, BUILD Ohio began as a 40-member
independent alliance of groups and individuals, many of whom served in
public-sector roles and all of whom were committed to working

collaboratively on behalf of young children and their families. It aligned the function of its work groups with an existing strategic framework that included 10-year goals and milestones. The focus was on three priority areas of professional development: standards and accountability, communications, and public will. Where BUILD Ohio focused on creating and strengthening the foundation and infrastructure of a comprehensive system (quality standards, professional development opportunities, and so on), advocacy campaigns focused on building public will and legislative awareness and support. Simultaneously, an inside-government group worked on identifying regulatory and policy changes necessary to effect long-term success.

When the next election ushered in a new era of gubernatorial attention to the state's youngest children, BUILD Ohio had helped lay a foundation upon which to build. The groundwork included achievements related to early learning and development standards, professional development, and placing priority on Ohio's Quality Rating and Improvement System, which had languished since its creation in 1999. In 2007, Ohio elected Governor Ted Strickland, who was outspoken in his commitment to education reform, beginning with early childhood. During his tenure, the QRIS, *Step up to Quality*, received $25 million in funding and the quality infrastructure described above was all in place.

Governor Strickland also established a new Early Childhood Cabinet to align state leadership, policy, and finance around a common goal of promoting school readiness for Ohio's children, prenatal to age 6. Even now, a decade later, Ohio's advances, led by its Early Childhood Advisory Council and the Race to the Top–Early Learning Challenge team, can be traced back to the quiet infrastructure development of the facilitative leadership group that reignited Ohio's early childhood systems-building. The Ohio experience illustrates that effective systems-building requires strategic thinking and systems leadership, which may emanate from leaders in diverse roles and often ones significantly less visible than the governor or even an agency director.

CONCLUSIONS

Leadership of early childhood systems-building requires an understanding of the breadth of an early childhood system and what is needed to bring it to fruition. The visionary leader can be catalytic, aligning efforts to bring reality more closely in line with an idea. When a vision is widely shared, it can serve as an umbrella under which previously disconnected leaders can find commonality and connection. It also serves as a set of parameters to guide opportunistic actions.

Effectively serving children, especially those who are at risk, requires a whole system, or a system of systems, approach. Because much of the early childhood field remains disconnected and because of the complexity and the primacy of connections (across sectors and systems) in systems-building, collaborative leaders, connectors, play a necessary and important role in systems change. The leaders with vision value, but may not possess, collaborative leadership.

Leaders of early childhood systems must be able to contend with multiple points of view and integrate those that diverge from their own. Participants in early childhood include legislators, legislative staff, advocates, small businesses, parents, pediatricians, school districts, principals, teachers, and others. Systems leaders must help develop and hold a vision that takes into account manifold interests, perspectives, and concerns. They must facilitate and support work with multiple stakeholders and focus on the connection between the vision and that stakeholder's intrinsic interest.

Leadership, or the lack thereof, is a convenient default explanation for why things did or did not occur (for example, the presence or absence of particular leadership was key). Yet leadership, as an explanation for success or failure, runs the risk of becoming a tautology, which tells us nothing. Clearly, leadership is essential to producing change, as many thinkers in the field have noted. But just as we lack in-depth analysis of governance, we also lack in-depth, field-based research on how leaders have created change and have been developed and supported.

As early childhood systems-building efforts continue to proliferate and strengthen, the need for greater theoretical clarity, policy-focused research, and on-the-ground experimentation will only grow. Leadership and governance are two critical areas of systems development worthy of significant additional investment and attention, as the stakes are raised and policymakers continue to demand evidence of results. Potential leaders need to be identified and developed. Current leaders need ongoing development and support, including peer networks and access to expertise. And stakeholders interested in advancing early childhood systems to improve outcomes for young children need research and analysis to help inform decisions about leadership supports and development efforts. Whether the context requires collaborative leadership or benefits from a charismatic or more top-down leader, we all know that *leadership matters*, and it matters a great deal. As the salience of early childhood increases, we have all the more reason to treat leadership in ways that acknowledge that truth.

REFERENCES

Beckwith, K. (2009). *BUILD Ohio case study: 2002–2008*. BUILD Initiative.

Bruner, C. (2003). *The Build Initiative: Building early learning systems in the states —A report on the first year*. Boston, MA: BUILD Initiative

Bruner, C. (2013a). *Top 10 things we know about young children and health equity . . . and three things we need to do with what we know*. Boston, MA: BUILD Initiative and Child and Family Policy Center.

Bruner, C. (2013b). *The BUILD Initiative resiliency and sustainability—Albert Einstein, governance, Margaret Mead, together we can, collective impact, geodesic networks, Anthony Downs, and next steps, 2012 national evaluation essay on the BUILD Initiative's contribution to state early childhood systems building*. Boston, MA: BUILD Initiative.

Bruner, C., Gebhard, B., & Hibbard, S. (2004). *Toward a theory of change for the BUILD Initiative: A discussion paper*. Boston, MA: BUILD Initiative.

Bruner, C., Wright, M. S., Gebhard, B., & Hibbard, S. (2004). *Building an early learning system: The ABCs of planning and governance structures* (State Early Childhood Policy Technical Assistance Network Resource Brief). Des Moines, IA: State Early Childhood Policy Technical Assistance Network (SECPTAN) and BUILD Initiative, c/o Child and Family Policy Center.

Coffman, J., Glazer, K., Hibbard, S., & Wiggins, K. (2010). *Early childhood system governance: Lessons from state experiences*. Boston, MA: BUILD Initiative.

Coffman, J., & Wright, M. S. (2011). *Developing leadership for early childhood systems building: Cross state evaluation brief*. Boston, MA: BUILD Initiative.

Early Childhood Funders Collaborative. (2002, January). [Mission statement]. Copy in possession of Susan Hibbard.

Fullan, M. (2002). Principals as leaders in a culture of change. *Educational Leadership, 59*(8), 16–21.

Goffin, S. G., & Lombardi, J. (1988). *Speaking out: Early childhood advocacy*. Washington, DC: NAEYC.

Goffin, S. G., & Washington, V. (2007). *Ready or not: Leadership choices in early care and education*. New York, NY: Teachers College Press.

NAEYC. (2012). *The Common Core State Standards: Caution and opportunity for early childhood education*. Washington, DC: National Association for the Education of Young Children.

Ochshorn, S. (2000). *Partnering for success: Community approaches to early learning*. New York, NY: Child Care Action Campaign.

Ponder, K. (2011). *Building early childhood systems: The collaborative leadership and accountability model*. Boston, MA: BUILD Initiative.

Shepard, L. A., Kagan, S. L., & Wurtz, E. O. (1998). *Principles and recommendations for early childhood assessments*. Washington, DC: National Education Goals Panel.

Stoney, L. (2013). *Shared services: A support strategy to Race to the Top–Early Learning Challenge*. Boston, MA: BUILD Initiative.

Stoney, L., & Blank, S. (2011). *Delivering quality: Strengthening the business side of early care and education*. Boston, MA: Opportunities Exchange.

CHAPTER 13

Revisiting Early Childhood Education's Governance Choices

Stacie G. Goffin and Beth Rous

As evidenced by this volume, governance of early childhood education (ECE) is becoming ever more complex as states and communities develop and implement new structures to oversee ECE components such as data systems, Quality Rating and Improvement Systems (QRIS), and prekindergarten to 3rd grade coordinated or integrated systems. Alongside this proliferation of ECE-related governance structures are public-private partnerships with diverse purposes, and advisory groups, such as State Advisory and Interagency Coordinating Councils, with responsibility for facilitating early childhood cross-sector activities.

States' identification of governance-related roles and responsibilities as part of their Race to the Top–Early Learning Challenge applications sheds light on the complexity presently characterizing ECE governance. A review of nine state submissions found on the BUILD Initiative website (buildinitiative.org) reveals that within each state, six to 14 state-level governance related entities coexist. Add to this landscape a lack of consensus on the role of governance and its functions (Goffin, Martella, & Coffman, 2011), and the plethora of organizations, structures, and purposes presently associated with ECE governance becomes apparent.

Few would use this reality, though, to justify retreating from governance as a crucial element of a well-functioning ECE system. Thus, it is timely to consider the consequences of choices made to date and to (1) revisit the question of government's responsibility in ECE, particularly as it relates to which ECE "parts" should fall under its purview, and (2) recognize capacity issues associated with increased visibility and politicization of ECE and the drive toward consolidated governance structures. Our intent in this chapter is to bring fresh thinking to the topic and catalyze further discussion.

OUR FRAMEWORK

We rely on a simple definition for governance: the action, manner, or system of governing. Concurring with Kagan and Kauerz (2009), authority and accountability are considered core governance features. Sidestepping the slippery slope on which programs and services reside within an ECE system, we see core features as applying to a system for children from birth to age 5 that incorporates programs and services most directly associated with the provision of ECE (prekindergarten, child care, Head Start, and early childhood–special education). Our choice of chronological scope rests on two premises: (1) Retaining the field's core values and diverse sectors is strengthened by a birth-to-5 scope, and (2) a coherent ECE system is essential for forging mutually needed connections between ECE and kindergarten–3rd grade.

Finally, although we are committed to approaches that facilitate coordinated support inclusive of children's health and welfare, we join with Kauerz and Kagan (2012) in arguing that governance of early childhood entities in service to this broad purpose should be viewed separately from ECE governance. Experience is teaching us that comprehensive early childhood systems development—and its governance—is fraught with issues of feasibility (Goffin, Martella, & Coffman, 2011). Further justification comes from the fact that results sought by these broad efforts depend on a well-formed and functioning ECE system (Goffin, 2012; Kagan, Goffin, Golub, & Pritchard, 1995).

GOVERNANCE OF ECE AS A FIELD OF PRACTICE

Kagan and Kauerz (2009) identified three phases of early childhood governance since the 1960s. The first phase focused on governance of individual programs and, although it was not the intention, intensified the field's fragmentation. In the mid-1980s and 1990s, governance efforts focused on facilitating cooperation and collaboration across programs and funding. This second phase led to various children's cabinets, state-level groups focused on collaboration, and public-private and state-local partnerships. Although they are still active as approaches, these entities typically lack the necessary authority to drive system coordination and alignment.

The first decade of the 21st century set the stage for the third—and current—governance phase. Governance today is characterized by increasing state and community involvement with early childhood comprehensive systems development and with organizational experimentation within ECE.

This includes creation of new stand-alone agencies, within-government consolidation, and colocated departments, each with the intent of better managing and monitoring early learning programs and services. Although they contribute to enhanced ECE management and coordination, these new structures are unlikely to have sufficient breadth to successfully unify ECE under a single mantle of authority and accountability.

Additionally, issues associated with program and system coordination and coherence now extend beyond policy, funding, and program delivery to include a myriad of coexisting community, regional, and state-level governance and quasi-governance entities. Given their quantity, ECE governance and its "assistive" organizations need to be recognized as a system with diverse functions operating with various levels of authority and accountability. It, too, needs linkages that promote coherence and accountability (Goffin, Martella, & Coffman, 2011).

This brief appraisal of Phase 3 ECE governance approaches suggests that a fourth phase may be warranted. We suggest that this fourth phase should have two priorities: (1) forging an appropriate relationship between ECE as a professional field of practice and government oversight of policy-related functions, and (2) developing management and leadership capacity to effectively use government authority and accountability to drive results. With self-governance (Priority 1), ECE would become more coherent and less politicized as a professional field of practice, and existing state, regional, and community approaches to governance could direct attention to responsibilities suitable to public governance structures—for example, aligning and coordinating state and federal policies, public financing, and programs and services supported by public funding. This would especially be the case if attention were also directed to the management and leadership capacity necessary to these tasks (Priority 2).

ECE AS A PROFESSIONAL FIELD OF PRACTICE

As the phases of governance outlined above make evident—and indicative of the field's growth in scale and prominence—governance efforts have repeatedly striven to resolve ECE's fragmentation. Most often, attention is focused on alleviating the disjuncture between and among policies, financing, and service delivery (Kagan, 1991; Kauerz & Kagan, 2012). Though professional development has long been recognized as an essential component of systems development, only recently has focused attention turned to the performance of ECE practitioners "on the ground." ECE's fragmentation as a *field of practice*—arguably representing ECE's core function and one central to establishing field-wide accountability—therefore represents a gaping void in discussions on governance. Further, given its centrality to competent performance, this void is best addressed by ECE as an organized field of practice.

Formation of ECE as a Professional Field of Practice

Aspirations of policymakers, philanthropists, business leaders, and, most important, families are unlikely to be fulfilled unless ECE addresses its competence as a field of practice and creates unified authority for practitioner preparation and standards of practice. In its absence:

- Too many children are losing ground and too many others cannot access their potential;
- Gains in scientific knowledge are neither widely understood nor consistently applied;
- Insufficient ability and capacity exists to respond to growing public expectations for ECE;
- Gains in credibility for ECE are not being transferred to the field's practitioners; and
- ECE is being redefined as a field of practice as others address its inadequacies (Goffin, 2013a).

The time has come for ECE to focus inwardly and to unify itself as a professional field of practice. Consistently high-quality ECE relies on the *collective* competence of its practitioners. Distinct from the ongoing debate about the value of degrees, organizing as a profession provides a field-unifying strategy that can establish an ECE *system* for preparation, practice, and accountability—a system that would be field-wide, would cohere the field's sectors and subsystems, and would be field-led (Goffin, 2013a).

As Rhodes and Huston (2012) argued, it is not sufficient to focus solely on professional development strategies to produce workforce competence. Evolving to a professional field of practice also necessitates professional regulation, that is, self-regulation/self-governance.

Yet presently, professional development is embedded in states' systems development activities and is situated as a domain for government oversight by state policymakers and agencies. Such an arrangement would be anathema to a profession. In the absence of organizing itself as a professional field of practice, ECE is largely delegating practitioner preparation and standard-setting functions to state government.

Although state regulation performs a crucial role in assuring the public that licensed individuals are at least minimally competent to perform their roles, by looking to public policy in the arena of professional development ECE has withdrawn from a profession's core duty to oversee use of its knowledge base and prepare practitioners accordingly, a duty uniformly recognized as a profession's obligation (Dower, O'Neil, & Hough, 2001; Freidson, 2001; Sullivan, 2005). By relying on policymakers to catalyze and approve field-wide change related to the practice of ECE, the field relinquishes a profession's core responsibility.

Professions are experiencing myriad changes in key areas such as financing and reduced professional independence; yet they maintain their distinctive occupational obligation: preparing individuals with specialized knowledge and the capability and autonomy to bring judgment to bear in its application, guided by a strong sense of public accountability (Freidson, 2001; Sullivan, 2005). ECE, as part of its movement toward professionalism, should assume responsibility via self-governance/professional regulation for application of its specialized knowledge by developing standards of practice, identifying competencies required for participation in the profession, and redesigning practitioner preparation.

Field-Wide Leadership for ECE

Reaching this milestone requires developing field-wide leadership. ECE has had many outstanding leaders. Its present status can largely be attributed to the efforts of these exceptional individuals. Advancing as a professionally competent field of practice, however, demands expanding beyond individual leadership and policy-driven change to developing field-wide leadership—collective action by ECE as a field of practice focused on advancing its capacity to higher levels of capability and competence (Dower, O'Neil, & Hough, 2001; Goffin, 2013a; Rhodes & Huston, 2012).

Professions assume this responsibility by setting standards of practice, establishing the competencies expected of individuals to achieve that standard and protect the public's welfare, designating the level of education necessary for achieving this result, and addressing issues that threaten the capacity to carry out a profession's mission (Schumann, 2013). Licensing and regulatory bodies, in turn, use professional standards and competencies to ensure competent performance does not fall below a designated minimum. Professions govern what defines them as a specialized field of practice. They—versus the state—drive performance expectations and ever-higher performance aspirations for their practitioners.

With the assistance of field-wide leadership, professions consciously and proactively attend to issues associated with a field's unity and collective competence. Although not immune to external forces, a profession's self-governance and field-wide leadership serve as a safeguard—and often a mediator—against arbitrary changes in preparation, practice, and professional accountability. Importantly, these expectations extend to all early educators, not just those whose programs receive public oversight because of their funding source.

Establishing ECE as a professional field of practice and developing the institutional capacity that undergirds the ability to be self-governing will require focused effort well into the mid-21st century. In the meantime, ECE should (1) critically assess the consequences of relinquishing authority and accountability for professional preparation and ongoing development to states and (2) carve out portable, state-driven strategies for advancing practitioners' competence so the field's present entrenchment in state policy doesn't further inhibit development as a profession. Organizing ECE as a professional field of practice will permit the scope of government agencies, advisory councils, and private-public partnerships at state, regional/county, and community levels to be reconfigured and their focus narrowed to functions more routinely associated with publicly funded governance bodies: coordinating disjointed public policies, increasing the efficiency of disconnected and overlapping delivery systems, policy implementation, and maximizing and monitoring the use of public financing.

MANAGEMENT AND LEADERSHIP FOR EFFECTIVE GOVERNANCE

In the interim, little attention has been paid to the fact that the field's present governance structures are as much about administering and managing ECE programs and services as they are about governance. Too often, the leadership and management infrastructure needed for individual and organizational effectiveness is overlooked. This oversight has resulted in limited attention being given to the knowledge and skills that those staffing ECE's governance structures need to achieve the outcomes assigned to them.

Distinguishing Leadership and Management

Though they sometimes overlap, leadership and management differ—a fact that is often overlooked. Failure to differentiate them can result in a misunderstanding of what is most needed for improving performance and/or effecting desired changes. Typically, management is defined as overseeing processes that keep a complicated system of people and technology running smoothly. This involves knowledge and skills related to planning, budgeting, organizing, staffing, and project management. Leadership attends to conditions for adapting to changing circumstances, recognizing opportunities for setting new direction, and navigating toward a different future. Involving a complex interplay of individual characteristics, context, specifics of a leadership issue, and key leadership behaviors (Goffin, 2013b), leadership frequently entails risk taking and mobilizing others to come together to realize a shared, often co-created vision.

Leadership and Management in Practice

State oversight of ECE programs traditionally has been dispersed across agencies. Those in these agencies with responsibilities for ECE programs and services most often bring programmatic knowledge and experience to their positions. The growing number, however, of stand-alone ECE and co-located agencies and consolidated divisions within existing state agencies has resulted in expanded government involvement, enlarged responsibilities, and increased organizational and political visibility, leading us to highlight the leadership and management expertise needed by those in positions within these new structures.

Growing attention to and increased politicization of ECE, along with calls for collaborative and integrated systems, has catalyzed the merger, co-location, and/or creation of new state-level departments and agencies. Although these changes in organization and governance are producing some of their intended advantages (simplified management and enhanced coordination), differences in organizational design create variations in what can be accomplished (Regenstein & Lipper, 2013). The diminishing number of agencies with oversight of ECE programs and services invites new challenges and seeds potential unintended consequences. Below, we describe two possible policy consequences that raise the importance of growing management and leadership capacity.

Traditionally, multiple agencies with oversight of ECE programs and services and the individuals across them have jointly engaged in decisionmaking. Though currently less prevalent, this approach arguably compensates for the natural ebb and flow of "strong" versus "weak" leadership and management within and across ECE sectors, because strength within and across agencies can vary from year to year. Consequently, poor leadership may affect one sector within ECE, while other ECE sectors function effectively. With a stand-alone, co-located, or consolidated structure, however, one "weak" link can have a detrimental domino effect on ECE's multiple sectors.

Another illustration of unintended consequences comes from the impact of staff changes at the highest levels (e.g., commissioners/secretaries) of state agencies in which ECE programs and services are located. Leadership changes at these levels often shift organizational agendas. Though leadership changes can be detrimental for any organization, political influences on leadership changes within state agencies can prove particularly consequential because of their frequency and their connection to policy agendas. These shifts can significantly affect, either positively or negatively, not only state-level policies, but also ECE programs and services.

These two illustrations demonstrate the stakes for ECE emanating from consolidated, co-located, and stand-alone agencies and the urgent need for capacity-building as it relates to the ECE personnel who work in these agencies. Within each of these governance structures, positive changes have the advantage of reaching multiple ECE programs and services—as do those changes associated with negative consequences. In contrast, in a decentralized state agency structure, positive and negative consequences tend to affect only targeted programs and services. When joined with the complexities created by governing the ECE-related components that comprise this volume and the myriad of community, regional, and state-level governance and quasi-governance entities, the need for greater leadership and management capacity becomes self-evident.

REDUCING THE LEADERSHIP-MANAGEMENT GAP

By their very nature, state agencies are complex bureaucracies. Further, demands are created when blending or creating a new organizational culture, developing new managerial systems, and responding to steeper accountability expectations. Regardless of one's position within an agency hierarchy—whether head of an agency or a department within an agency, or something in between—those in these positions (which typically receive the label of leadership positions) are called upon to exercise the leadership and management required to fulfill the intentions of the new agencies, departments, and divisions.

Leadership and management knowledge and skills fall under four organizational "frames": structural, human resource, symbolic, and political (Bolman & Deal, 2008). These frames encompass familiarity with the rules, roles, goals, policies, and environment within one's agency; the knowledge necessary to determine what is organizationally feasible; the capacity to hire competent staff, empower them to contribute to agency goals, and deepen and broaden individual and collective competence; attention to organizational culture and climate—the invisible web that drives commitment to an agency and its purpose; and finally, the ability to negotiate power, conflict, and politics revolving around decisionmaking regarding who gets what, when, and how (Lasswell, 1972).

Using this framework, leaders and managers are needed who are:

1. Analysts and architects of effective organizational environments that support and promote the field's agenda;
2. Catalysts for change and growth;
3. Motivators who inspire those contributing to organizational goals; and
4. Advocates and negotiators.

The leadership-management gap can be reduced by developing these capacities in state agencies responsible for governing ECE.

CONCLUSIONS: LOOKING FORWARD

ECE is in the midst of dramatic change. Eagerness to reduce the field's fragmentation has led to state-level structures in various forms. This volume offers the opportunity to contemplate the consequences of choices made thus far in the realm of ECE governance. We would suggest that, to date, one of the most significant consequences is the more visible role given to government and state departments of education in relation to ECE, in conjunction with increased attention to the execution and management of ECE programs. Looking ahead, questions remain regarding the impact of the increasing governance role being given to state boards of education and other entities assuming greater influence over ECE, especially in light of the fact that ECE is but one of numerous issues under their purview.

This has led us to conclude that a next phase of thinking about ECE governance is warranted, one that attends to consequences of recent choices: the need for ECE to (1) develop a unified structure/process for governing itself as a professional field of practice and (2) address the growing leadership and management demands being placed on ECE personnel within state agencies overseeing ECE programs and services.

The first recommendation is one that requires ECE to step forward and assume responsibility for its collective competence. It will require sustained "internal" as well as external public will to come to fruition. Though effective governance might be possible without ECE organizing itself as a professional field of practice, it would be accomplished through ECE's continued absorption by federal and state government bureaucracies, which would not only further subject the field to the political and often uninformed whims of governance but would also reduce ECE's opportunity to be recognized as a profession with oversight for the development and use of its specialized expertise on behalf of children's early care and education.

The second recommendation is more amenable to near-term action plans for implementation. Early learning administrators in state education and early learning agencies are being asked to navigate a changing educational context that is increasingly politicized. They are:

- Experiencing sharp shifts in their organizational context;
- Being asked to attend not only to the efficacy of programs under their purview but also to effect system changes within and across state agencies;
- Being asked to expand their content knowledge and skills;
- Expected to develop working relationships with K–3 colleagues;
- Expected to learn how to navigate cross-agency relationships and change; and
- Being asked to expand their responsibilities to include both program oversight and the exercise of leadership (Goffin, 2013b).

Collectively, these new realities intensify the need for systematic leadership and management development.

This chapter calls for a fourth phase of ECE governance development, one defined by different thinking. We recognize that our recommendations may not be the ones anticipated. We believe, however, that the choices made to date call for more *systemic* thinking to be brought to bear on governing ECE.

REFERENCES

Bolman, L. G., & Deal, T. E. (2008). *Reframing organizations: Artistry, choice, and leadership* (4th ed.). San Francisco, CA: Jossey-Bass.

Dower, C., O'Neil, E., & Hough, H. J. (2001, September). *Profiling the professions: A model for evaluating emerging health professions.* San Francisco, CA: Center for the Health Professions, University of California–San Francisco. Retrieved from www.soundrock.com/sop/pdf/Profiling%20tg%200Professions.pdf

Freidson, E. (2001). *Professionalism: The third logic.* Chicago, IL: The University of Chicago Press.

Goffin, S. G. (2009). *Field-wide leadership: Insights from five fields of practice.* Washington, DC: Goffin Strategy Group. Retrieved from https://a20f3032-a-62cb3a1a-s-sites.googlegroups.com/site/goffinstrategygroup/docu/

Field-WideLeadership_Final.pdf?attachauth=ANoY7crNBvd054oSIweFMXup-
R7YIdReexYNwIdUx5pR7OkNKEXfQqGKLPbJifu8Dg2PbosE13suU7SG
DwOKs16yugPZI8fSlmHhjToadA5LJmLPPhyCz1cggv3d5N93oEojkt5fepm-
RCbYQH_wWWac3bLnFxoeTd2r9ELPEAI-URPS31m8mIjbQkqFaDqg-
wZON60TAMoqPs0S-8ZuObcJ-eY5CpMocSQVo_7oIiiWV6PwRNA_
F6L5sF19KEPN55IfPUBo0WO3-ct&attredirects=0
Goffin, S. G. (2012). Beyond systemic structures: Penetrating to the core of an early
    care and education system. In S. L. Kagan & K. Kauerz (Eds.), *Early childhood
    systems: Transforming early learning* (pp. 267–282). New York, NY: Teachers
    College Press.
Goffin, S. G. (2013a). *Early childhood education for a new era: Leading for our
    profession*. New York, NY: Teachers College Press.
Goffin, S. G. (2013b). *Building capacity through an early education leadership
    academy*. Paper commissioned by the Center on Enhancing Early Learning
    Outcomes (CEELO). Retrieved from www.goffinstrategygroup.com & http://
    ceelo.org/wp-content/uploads/2013/12/EELA_Goffin_WEB.pdf
Goffin, S. G., Martella, J., & Coffman, J. (2011). *Vision to practice: Setting a new
    course for early childhood governance*. Washington, DC: Goffin Strategy Group.
Kagan, S. L. (1991). *United we stand: Collaboration for child care and early educa-
    tion services*. New York, NY: Teachers College Press.
Kagan, S. L., Goffin, S. G., Golub, S. A., & Pritchard, E. (1995). *Toward systemic
    reform: Service integration for young children and their families*. Falls Church,
    VA: National Center for Service Integration.
Kagan, S. L., & Kauerz, K. (2009). Governing American early care and educa-
    tion: Shifting from government to governance and from form to function. In
    S. Feeney, A. Galper, & C. Seefeldt (Eds.), *Continuing issues in early childhood
    education* (3rd ed., pp. 12–32). Columbus, OH: Pearson Merrill Prentice Hall.
Kauerz, K., & Kagan, S. L. (2012). Governance and early childhood systems:
    Different forms, similar goals. In S. L. Kagan & K. Kauerz (Eds.), *Early child-
    hood systems: Transforming early learning* (pp. 87–103). New York, NY:
    Teachers College Press.
Lasswell, H. (1972). *Politics: Who gets what, when, and how*. New York, NY: A
    Meridian/World Publishing/Times Mirror.
Regenstein, E., & Lipper, K. (2013). *A framework for choosing a state-level ear-
    ly childhood governance structure*. Retrieved from www.buildinitiative.org/
    WhatsNew/ViewArticle/tabid/96/ArticleId/628/A-Framework-for-Choosing-a-
    State-Level-Early-Childhood-Governance-System.aspx
Rhodes, H., & Huston, A. (2012). Building the workforce our youngest children
    deserve. *Social Policy Report, 26*(1), 3–26.
Schumann, M. J. (2013). Foreword. In S. G. Goffin, *Early childhood education for
    a new era: Leading for our profession* (pp. xi–xiv). New York, NY: Teachers
    College Press.
Sullivan, W. M. (2005). Markets vs. professions: Value added? *Daedalus, 134*(3),
    19–26.

Early Childhood Governance
Present and Prospective Views

Rebecca E. Gomez and Sharon Lynn Kagan

As we noted at the outset of this volume, one of the goals of creating a volume on early childhood governance was to illustrate the nascent and diverse status of thinking about what constitutes "governance" and its role in shaping the field of early childhood education (ECE). In this epilogue, we coalesce some of the thinking presented herein and consider some options for the future.

EARLY CHILDHOOD GOVERNANCE: PRESENT VIEWS

If nothing else, this volume crystallizes the fact that the governance of early childhood education is complex. This complexity is derived from, as we discussed in Part I, Chapter 1 (Kagan), the fact that a state's approach to governance evolves out of its unique and storied history, political climate, social culture, and values about services for young children and their families. As was illustrated in Part II of the volume by Regenstein, Gomez, and Dichter, there are many approaches to governance; indeed, even among states that have chosen to enact similar forms of governance, the functions accorded the governance approaches vary. Implementing governance approaches is not a small endeavor; they take political, intellectual, and financial investment. These chapters suggest, however, that investing human and fiscal capital in governance influences the way that ECE systems are evolving.

The contributions showcased in Part III of the volume provide insight into the complex relationship between governance and the other ECE system elements. In addition to discussing the relationship between governance and a particular system element in depth, these chapters reveal that governance decisions can and have had an important influence on systems development. Chapters 5 (Tarrant and Schaack) and 10 (LeMoine), for instance, discuss the implications that particular forms and functions of governance have had on QRIS and professional development subsystems; while Chapters 6 (Scott-Little), 7 (Schultz), and 11 (Rendon) yield important insights into the fact that governance is not static, but a collection of processes that evolve over time; these processes engage the ECE field in developing critical system elements such as standards, accountability mechanisms, and opportunities for family and community outreach. Chapters 8 (Cochenour and Hebbeler) and 9 (Grafwallner) suggest that data and financing undergird all aspects of an ECE system, and that effective governance of these policy domains requires both intentionality and innovation.

Part IV adds to our understanding of the complexity of governance, as it is addressed conceptually by Hibbard and Goffin and Rous. Hibbard's chapter asks us to extend our understanding of governance beyond a collection of policy structures and processes, and to move toward conceptualizing governance as a process that is inextricably intertwined with the development and selection of ECE leaders. Goffin and Rous ask us to ponder, in a field that is still grappling with its own identity, whether a focus on governance provides an opportunity to develop mechanisms for self-governance, rather than relying on extant structures, definitions, or beliefs to achieve effective governance of the *field* of ECE.

In sum, we now have a clearer picture of the complexities associated with governance, as well as with its multiple evolutions. These imply that governance, though here to stay, is likely to remain both highly idiosyncratic and individualized. Ideas about easy replication have given way to more detailed strategies of adaptation.

EARLY CHILDHOOD GOVERNANCE: PROSPECTIVE VIEWS

Despite the diversity in definitions of form and function, of conceptualizations of governance type, and in who or what entities could/should have authority over early childhood for a particular state or nation discussed in this volume, we render two recommendations to consider when thinking about the next steps for ECE governance.

First, we need to develop clear expectations for what governance can and cannot accomplish. Much of the work to date and the work presented in this volume has focused on the inputs of governance, notably its forms and functions, but very little has focused on its outcomes. To the degree that outcomes are being considered, governance expectations can be quite broad and quite high, with some suggesting that governance is not only a panacea for redressing the uncoordinated ECE delivery system, but that it can also produce improved child and family outcomes. Kagan, however, suggests that good governance has the potential to impact three systemic outputs: more equitable distribution of services, improved quality of services, and enhanced sustainability of services. These outputs are presented as interim achievements that are necessary precursors to achieving improved outcomes for all children and families. As interim outputs, they become the necessary and measurable elixirs to achievable outcomes for children and families, but governance cannot be held solely accountable for achieving child outcomes. Governance is too far removed from children and families, with hosts of intervening variables (e.g., family functioning, family economy) carrying much of the outcome burden. As a result, it would be both difficult and unwise to attempt to attribute causality for learning and development outcomes to the creation and implementation of governance mechanisms. Rather, governance should be regarded as a much-needed infrastructural element of the ECE system, one that ideally authorizes and oversees other systemic interventions designed for improving child outcomes (e.g., QRIS, standards, professional development).

Second, and once the outputs of governance are clarified, policymakers and scholars must develop a coherent strategy for evaluating the process and effects of ECE governance efforts to date. Although we do share the results of one qualitative study that examined the relationship between governance and ECE system coherence in two states (Gomez), much more research needs to be conducted on the opportunities and limits of governance for impacting ECE system development. As states undertake the work of developing ECE governance approaches, they are doing so without a strong research base to guide them. Allowing this to persist deters them from using important information to guide important decisions.

CONCLUSIONS

A myriad of opinions exist about the purpose and effectiveness of focusing on governance. Perhaps the only area of consensus regarding governance is that it is a timely topic. Given its temporal salience, this volume offers both theoretical and practical perspectives on how governance can impact systems development, potentially rendering ECE systems more coherent and effective in their goal of producing equitably distributed, high-quality, and sustainable ECE systems. It is to that end that this volume is dedicated.

About the Contributors

Sharon Lynn Kagan, EdD, is the Virginia and Leonard Marx Professor of Early Childhood and Family Policy, codirector of the National Center for Children and Families at Teachers College, Columbia University, and professor adjunct at Yale University's Child Study Center. Recognized nationally and internationally for her accomplishments related to the care and education of young children, Kagan is a prolific public speaker, author of 300 articles and 14 books, a member of more than 30 national boards or panels, and is working with countries around the globe to establish early learning standards, public policies, and teacher education strategies. Recipient of national and international honorary doctoral degrees, Kagan is past president of the National Association for the Education of Young Children and a past president of Family Support America. She has served as chair of the National Education Goals Panel Technical Planning Group for Goal One; a member of the Clinton Education Transition Team; a Distinguished Fellow for the Education Commission of the States; and a member of numerous National Academy of Sciences, foundation, and administration panels. She was made a fellow of the American Educational Research Association (AERA) in 2010 and elected to membership in the National Academy of Education in 2012. She is the only woman in the history of American education to receive its three most prestigious awards: the 2004 Distinguished Service Award from the Council of Chief State School Officers (CCSSO), the 2005 James Bryant Conant Award for Lifetime Service to Education from the Education Commission of the States (ECS), and the Harold W. McGraw Jr. Prize in Education.

Rebecca E. Gomez, EdD, holds the Rauch Postdoctoral Fellowship at the National Center for Children and Families (NCCF), Teachers College, Columbia University. Her research interests include exploring the impact of state-level governance on early childhood systems, the impact of professional development systems on improving workforce quality and stability, and multilevel governance approaches in early childhood. Some of the studies in which Gomez has participated include analyses on the effect of governance on state-level systems-building for a number of U.S. states, on the availability and quality of services for young children and their families on Long Island, on states' early learning standards, and on the impact of professional development systems on improving teacher qualifications across a number of countries. Before joining NCCF, Gomez worked for a variety of state and national early childhood organizations, including the Pennsylvania Early Learning Keys to Quality program, NACCRRA, and the State of New Hampshire's Child Development Bureau. She has also held adjunct faculty positions in the Early Childhood departments at West Chester University and Granite State College. She earned her MEd in Early Childhood from the University of New Hampshire in 2004, and her BA in American Studies from Rutgers University in 2001. She was named a Children's Defense Fund Emerging Leader in 2004 and a NACCRRA Emerging Leader in 2005. She is a former member of the Commonwealth of Pennsylvania's Early Learning Council and the NAEYC Governing Board.

Missy Cochenour is the program manager and early childhood integrated data system expert at Applied Engineering Management (AEM). She specializes in using data from local, state, and federal agencies to inform decisions in early childhood. Through the Statewide Longitudinal Data System (SLDS) State Support Team (SST) and the IDEA Center on Early Childhood Data Systems (DaSy), she currently provides technical assistance to states on integrating early childhood data and leads the early learning team on the Common Education Data Standards. Her experience ranges from local Head Start and State Preschool programs to federal policy and technical assistance. She received a BA in Education from the University of Redlands, an MA in Policy Evaluation from Claremont Graduate School, and is currently working on her PhD at George Mason University.

Harriet Dichter served as Pennsylvania's founding deputy secretary, Office of Child Development and Early Learning, where she gained national attention for the state's unique solutions and partnerships. Dichter's diverse action-oriented leadership has included foundations (Pew Trusts, Gates and Ford Foundations); the public sector (executive director, Delaware Office of Early Learning; Maternal and Child Health director and deputy managing director, Children's Policy, city of Philadelphia); and child policy and advocacy with community, state, and national nonprofits (United Way, Ounce of Prevention Fund, and its federal policy and advocacy affiliate, the First Five Years Fund). She is a graduate of Yale University, summa cum laude, and the University of Pennsylvania Law School, cum laude.

Stacie G. Goffin, EdD, is principal of the Goffin Strategy Group. Established in 2004, the Goffin Strategy Group dedicates itself to building early childhood education's ability to provide effective programs and services for young children through leadership, capacity, and systems development. Goffin works with local and state nonprofits, governments, national organizations, and philanthropy. A widely published author, Goffin's conceptual leadership focuses on advancing early childhood education as a professional field of practice. Prior to forming the Goffin Strategy Group, Goffin led the 5-year effort to redesign the National Association for the Education of Young Children's (NAEYC) early childhood program accreditation system. She is a former senior program officer at the Ewing Marion Kauffman Foundation, higher education faculty member, and preschool educator. More information can be found at www.goffinstrategygroup.com.

Rolf Grafwallner is the assistant state superintendent of the Division of Early Childhood Development at the Maryland State Department of Education. The division is responsible for state policy and the technical support for all early childhood programs serving children, birth through kindergarten. He has 30 years of experience in early childhood education as a teacher, program manager, and state administrator. He received an MA in Political Science from the University of Munich, Germany, an MA in Education for Early Childhood/Elementary Education from Millersville University, Pennsylvania, and a PhD from the University of Maryland–College Park in the area of Education Policy, Planning, and Administration. Dr. Grafwallner was instrumental in 2000 in developing a statewide kindergarten assessment, the first of its kind in the country. He assisted in developing policies for all-day kindergarten for all 5-year-olds and the expansion of prekindergarten programs to all 4-year-olds who are economically disadvantaged. He led efforts to consolidate all early care and education programs into Maryland's State Department of Education, thereby creating a new governance model for early childhood education nationally.

Kathleen Hebbeler is a program manager at SRI International where she oversees research, evaluation, and technical assistance projects focused on improving services and supports for young children and their families. She has directed large-scale projects involving quantitative and qualitative methods for federal and state agencies and private foundations. Currently, Dr. Hebbeler directs the IDEA Center on Early Childhood Data Systems (DaSy), which provides technical assistance to early intervention and early childhood special education state agencies to improve data systems and data quality. Previously, she directed the Early Childhood Outcomes (ECO) Center, which was a 10-year effort to build the capacity of states to report high-quality data on child and family outcomes. Dr. Hebbeler earned her PhD in human development and family studies from Cornell University.

Susan Hibbard has worked for the BUILD Initiative since it was launched in 2002. She currently serves as its Executive Director. BUILD is a national project that supports state efforts to create comprehensive early childhood systems—coordinated, effective policies that address children's health, mental health and nutrition, early care and education, family support and parenting programs, and services for children with special needs. In this capacity, she oversees the Learning Community and works to connect state leaders from the public and private sector to share strategies and information and fosters development of a supportive leadership and knowledge network. The initiative supports efforts to re-form existing state systems, test new models, and connect programs and services that now operate in isolation and sometimes at cross-purposes and help ensure that all young children have access to early learning systems that result in school readiness. Hibbard leads BUILD efforts to maximize federal early childhood initiatives including through the Early Learning Challenge Collaborative, which supported state leaders as they applied for, and now as they implement, the federal Race to the Top-Early Learning Challenge grant plans—with or without federal funding. Hibbard also leads BUILD's support of the Early Childhood Funders' Collaborative.

Sarah LeMoine's work over the past 25 years has focused primarily on early childhood professional development systems and activities, workforce diversity, and leadership issues. She holds an MS in leadership and policy from Wheelock College and has extensive experience ranging from direct service work to national-level research and writing, technical assistance (TA) and training, policy analysis, and advocacy. Currently, Ms. LeMoine serves as the project director for the National Center on Child Care Professional Development Systems and Workforce Initiatives (PDW Center) at ZERO TO THREE, which is jointly funded by the Administration for Children and Families' Office of Child Care and Office of Head Start. Prior to directing the PDW Center, Ms. LeMoine was NAEYC's director of State Workforce Systems Policy. She also previously held the positions of TA manager, Information Services manager, and researcher/writer for the National Child Care Information and Technical Assistance Center (NCCIC); and conducted research and TA at the Wheelock College Center for Career Development. Ms. LeMoine has authored/co-developed numerous professional development systems publications and tools, including NAEYC's and NACCRRA's Training and TA Glossary; NAEYC's Policy Blueprint; NCCIC's simplified systems model, referred to as "the tree" and the related toolkit; and the first national TA paper on cross-sector PD systems.

Elliot Regenstein leads the Ounce of Prevention Fund's national policy consultation practice and coordinates its overall state and national policy efforts. He has extensive experience in working directly with states on policy development and is a frequent speaker and author on topics that include governance, data systems, and linkages between early learning and K–12. He also partners with the First Five Years Fund to support policy change at the federal level. Regenstein was one of the chief architects of Illinois' 2006 Preschool for All program while serving in the governor's office as director of education reform. Regenstein cochaired the Illinois Early Learning Council from 2004 until April 2009 and currently serves as a member of the Council's Executive Committee, cochairing its Data, Research, and Evaluation Committee. He holds a BA in History from Columbia University and a law degree from the University of Michigan. After law school, he served as a clerk to the Honorable Kenneth F. Ripple on the U.S. Court of Appeals for the Seventh Circuit.

Thomas Rendon is the coordinator of the Iowa Head Start State Collaboration Office at the Iowa Department of Education. His office is responsible for designing and supporting various Head Start collaboration initiatives which include T.E.A.C.H., Positive Behavioral Interventions and Supports, Multi-Tiered Systems of Support, Head Start–Pre-K Collaboration, oral health services, and leadership in the state's Early Childhood Advisory Committee. He spearheaded the Iowa's first Parent Summit and developed a statewide training on cultural competence for early childhood professionals. He currently serves as treasurer of the Iowa Association for the Education of Young Children and also is vice president of the Iowa subdivision of the Division of Early Childhood, Council of Exceptional Children. He has a BS in Speech from Northwestern University and an MBA from the University of Iowa, and is working on a PhD from Kent State University.

Beth Rous is professor and chair of the Department of Educational Leadership Studies at the University of Kentucky. She serves as director of the Kentucky Partnership for Early Childhood Services at the Human Development Institute at the University of Kentucky. Dr. Rous's primary interest is the intersection between child care, early intervention, early childhood special education, Head Start, and public prekindergarten programs. Her research and scholarship has focused on three major areas: (1) transition of young children between and among early childhood systems; (2) state standards and accountability systems; and (3) quality of workforce and service systems. She has served as a consultant and/or advisor on numerous national studies such as the State and Local Implementation of IDEA and

Pre-Elementary Education Longitudinal Studies, and served as principal investigator for the National Early Childhood Transition Research Center.

Diana Schaack, Ph.D, is an assistant professor of Child and Family Development at San Diego State University (SDSU). Her research focuses on measuring early care and education quality, effective interventions to improve ECE quality, and the psychological well-being of the workforce and its relationships to the quality of teacher-child attachment relationships and children's emotional development. Prior to joining SDSU, Dr. Schaack provided technical assistance to states building QRIS and worked at Qualistar Early Learning where she helped develop, implement, and evaluate Colorado's QRIS.

Thomas Schultz is project director for Early Childhood Initiatives at the Council of Chief State School Officers (CCSSO) in Washington, DC, where he works with states to improve learning opportunities and outcomes for young children. Prior to joining the Council, Dr. Schultz worked at the Pew Charitable Trusts, where he coauthored *Taking Stock: Assessing and Improving Early Childhood Learning and Program Quality*, based on the work of the National Early Childhood Accountability Task Force. From 1995 to 2005, he served as a senior manager in the Head Start Bureau, where he led initiatives in the areas of child assessment, program evaluation, professional development, and collaboration with other early care and education programs. He has also worked in the U.S. Department of Education as a research manager, as an early childhood project director with the National Association of State Boards of Education, as a Head Start Program team leader in the Region V Office of Child Development, and a teacher in the Chicago Public Schools. He is a graduate of Oberlin College and the Harvard Graduate School of Education.

Catherine Scott-Little, PhD, is currently an associate professor in the Department of Human Development and Family Studies at the University of North Carolina at Greensboro. Working with Sharon Lynn Kagan and other colleagues at Teachers College, Scott-Little has completed several national studies on state-level early learning and development standards (ELDS), including a content analysis of 46 preschool ELDS and a second project that analyzed the content of infant-toddler early learning guidelines. She has served as an advisor on ELDS in numerous states. Scott-Little completed her undergraduate degree in Child and Family Development at the University of North Carolina at Greensboro and a doctorate degree in Human Development at the University of Maryland at College Park. She worked as a deputy director of a large Head Start program and served as the director of the Expanded Learning Opportunities Project at the SERVE Center prior to joining the Human Development and Family Studies faculty.

Kate Tarrant is an independent early childhood research and policy consultant whose clients include the BUILD Initiative, New York State's Early Childhood Advisory Council, AIR, and other national, state, and local organizations. Tarrant earned a doctorate in education from Teachers College, Columbia University, where she also served as a graduate research fellow at the National Center for Children and Families. She received a BA from Emory University and an MPA from Columbia University's School of International and Public Affairs. She coauthored a book on the early care and education workforce, coedited a volume on early childhood transitions and alignment, and has written numerous book chapters, reports, and journal articles. Her work focuses on comprehensive early childhood systems, workforce development, and quality improvement policy.

Index